THE SEVEN PRINCIPLES
OF
PROFESSIONAL SERVICES

*A field guide for successfully walking
the consulting tightrope*

SHANE ANASTASI

W W W . P S P R I N C I P L E S . C O M

This publication is designed to provide accurate and authoritative information in regard to the subject matter covered. It is sold with the understanding that the publisher and author are not engaged in rendering legal or accounting services. If legal advice or other expert assistance is required, the services of a competent professional should be sought.

Copyright © 2014 Shane Anastasi

Published by PS Principles
www.psprinciples.com

Front Cover Image "Businessman in equilibrium on a rope over a cityscape" Copyright Ollyy, used under license from Shutterstock.com

Library of Congress Control Number: 2014958202

PS Principles, Chicago IL

Publisher: PS Principles

Editor: Thomas McGrath

Cover Designer: Shane Anastasi

ISBN: 978-0-9862107-0-9

10 9 8 7 6 5 4 3 2 1

1. Business 2. Education

First Edition

Printed by CreateSpace, an Amazon Company

To Mary, Audrey, Tess and James:

It is your amazing love and support that gets me through each day.

Without it, I'd be lost.

- Shane

CONTENTS

Acknowledgements 1

Foreword 3

Introducing the Seven Principles 7
A Common Tale of Woe 7
The Need for Balance 12
It is a Dangerous Tightrope 14
Accelerating a Consultant's Learning Curve 16
Maintaining Balance with Principles 18
Learn from Other People's Experiences 20
Why Get Better at Walking the Tightrope? 21
Nobody is Perfect 22

Principle No. 1: Adapt to Your Environment 25
Success from Adaptation 25
Understanding the Engagement Environment 27
The Basic Dynamics of an Engagement Environment 47
Adapting to the Engagement Environment 52
Chapter Summary 59

Principle No. 2: Always Know What *Done* Looks Like 61
Visualizing the Outcome 61
The Contract: The First Version of *Done* 65
What if There is No Contract? 70
Field Example: Starting Without a Contract 75
Prescribing *Done* 77
Field Example: Prescribing *Done* 78
Changing *Done*: Baselines and Change Management 81
Preparing to be *Done* – Customer Acceptance Testing 86
Leveraging Acceptance 91
Field Example: Nobody Knew What *Done* Looked Like! 93
Chapter Summary 97

Principle No. 3: Manage Expectations 99
Great Expectations 99
Managing Inherent Expectations 101
Balancing Expectations: The Triple Constraints 104
Field Example: Misaligned from the Beginning 109

How Do Expectations Become Misaligned? 114

Field Example: TICK-TICK-TICK-BOOM! 119

Who, What, When and the Three Hows 123

The Importance of Estimates 126

Chapter Summary 128

Principle No. 4: Have Difficult Conversations Early 131

Step Up to the Plate 131

The Cost of Doing Nothing 133

The Distraction of Urgency 138

Is it My Job to Have Difficult Conversations? 139

Getting Your Head Right 145

Empathy, Understanding and Resolution 151

Selling the Resolution 158

Really Difficult Conversations 160

Field Example: Tying it All Together 163

Chapter Summary 170

Principle No. 5: Think F.A.A.S.T. 171

Keep Calm and Carry On 171

Turning Quality into a Habit 172

Thinking F.A.A.S.T. 174

Focus 175

Attention to Detail 176

Accountable 179

Skilled 182

Trustworthy 183

Field Example: Crisis Mode 187

Chapter Summary 191

Principle No. 6: Participate in the Collective Wisdom 193

What is Collective Wisdom? 193

The Benefits of Using Collective Wisdom 196

You and the Collective Wisdom 198

Unpredictable Reactions to the Collective Wisdom 199

Field Example: Prescribing the Collective Wisdom 200

Contributing to the Collective Wisdom 203

An Introduction to Intellectual Property 204

Chapter Summary 211

Principle No. 7: Stay Engaged — 213

You Only Have One Career — 213
The Generic Professional Services Career Map — 215
The Professional Services Career Stages — 220
Engaging with Your Career — 227
Understanding Salary Increases — 234
Field Example: A Real Life Career Path — 239
Chapter Summary — 242

Conclusion: This is Only the Beginning — 245

ACKNOWLEDGEMENTS

I would like to warmly acknowledge the help of my colleagues who reviewed this text and acted as my own group of trusted advisors. Some of them even contributed their own experiences so that others could learn from them. It is your stories that bring the principles to life. It was a pleasure working with you, and it would be a privilege to do so again. Thank you.

Godard Abel	CEO SteelBrick and Co-founder G2 Crowd
Devang Bhavsar	VP of Professional Services, Personify Scrum Master
Craig Broadbent	CEO Stonebridge Systems
Matt Gorniak	CRO at SteelBrick & Director at G2 Crowd
Nick Jones	Director of Global Services at OpenText
Michael Martin	Senior Enterprise Architect at CirrusCPQ
Gavin McCloskey	Digital Media Architect at Telstra Australia
John Pora	VP of Professional Services at Aria Systems Project Management Professional
Erich Rusch	Co-Founder of CirrusCPQ and; CEO and Co-Founder of Sprockit
Jeffrey Wells	IBM Professional Services Executive Certified PMP & Muscle Car Enthusiast

FOREWORD

Godard Abel

Serial Entrepreneur (BigMachines, SteelBrick, G2Crowd)

For 20 years, I have either worked in or led many different professional services organizations. The principles defined in this book remind me of many of the lessons I learned at McKinsey, where I worked after being hired as a management consultant in 1994, fresh out of engineering school at MIT. Like many junior consultants, I was highly motivated as a problem-solver, but I lacked an understanding of our clients' organizational dynamics, and I did not know how to manage their expectations. After three years of learning at McKinsey, I returned to business school at Stanford, which led me down the route of becoming an enterprise software entrepreneur. From this vantage point, I have seen firsthand the impact a well-run professional services team has on the success of a company and its clients.

I first got to know Shane when I was the CEO of BigMachines, which was fast becoming the leading provider of cloud-based CPQ (configure, price, quote) software. After starting the company in 2000 and spending a few years struggling to find the right product-market fit, we had finally entered the "tornado" of rapid growth. BigMachines had become the world's leading cloud CPQ company, and it was becoming obvious that the biggest inhibitor to continued growth was our ability to implement our own software into enterprise IT environments.

When Shane joined us, we were close to doubling our yearly bookings for four consecutive years, and we were facing substantial challenges in scaling our professional services to keep up with the accelerating demand. We were starting to win many large enterprise accounts that required extensive implementation services. This kind of complex implementation required a different level of service provision than what we had been successfully delivering to smaller mid-market companies.

We had hired many talented and committed young professional services consultants with tremendous technical aptitude and product knowledge. Unfortunately, they also lacked experience in communicating with enterprise customers during their large, high-pressured and complex projects. Our team was becoming strained, and we were fighting many "fires" across a rapidly growing portfolio of hundreds of new implementation and add-on projects. Many of the projects were not getting *done* on schedule, which was leading to an ever-growing backlog of open projects that were in the process of escalating. Our customers were counting on us to automate their mission-critical quoting and ordering processes, and thus our project delays often led to difficult conversations with stressed and unhappy customers. Our growing portfolio of escalating projects was inhibiting the growth of my software company.

To complicate matters, a substantial re-capitalization of $80M in new capital from new investors shifted our professional services objectives. This injection of new capital also came with new expectations, which included the desire for our services team to begin generating profit. Our increasing escalations had forced our professional service's margin into the negative and this began to threaten our continued growth. We had to widen our focus from just services scalability so that it now included the additive goal of driving substantial services margins despite a backlog of unprofitable projects.

By being straightforward with our clients in a manner that earned their trust and respect, Shane enabled us to weather this storm by staying calm amidst the many fires and by always being straightforward with our clients. On numerous occasions, Shane had many difficult conversations with customers, and he frequently helped to reset their expectations toward a mutual vision of what *done* should look like. He then had to convince each customer that moving to this new vision of *done* was a good outcome despite the over inflated expectations they currently possessed. More impressively, Shane accomplished all this while simultaneously teaching our young professional service managers and team members the framework of "Shane-isms" spelled out in this book.

Under Shane's leadership, the services team regained control of the project portfolio, so that the company could continue to grow rapidly and profitably. BigMachines was ultimately acquired by Oracle in 2013, resulting in an excellent outcome for the investors. Clearly, Shane's influence helped shape this result.

Recently, I became CEO of another next generation CPQ company called SteelBrick. Our professional services team is now composed of many team members who were part of Shane's team at BigMachines, where they clearly learned these principles and matured as managers. Just the other day, I was in our conference room and witnessed our Director of Professional Services mentoring a newly hired consultant by spelling out the "ABCs" of professional services on a white-board. As you will read, this Director acquired this knowledge while working for Shane, and it is incredibly comforting for me to know that my current head of professional services has absorbed many of

Shane's principles. I will always want my most senior professional services executive to embrace these principles and employ them to the benefit of my companies. Deploying such a concise and effective framework of principles provides me with the confidence that we are delivering the right balance of company and customer success.

By providing a common method and language, distilled from years of experience, I believe this book is a valuable tool for scaling enterprise-grade professional service teams. Ideally, it will help create an environment where consultants won't have to learn their wisdom by making costly and damaging mistakes. I am also thrilled that Shane, who has become a personal friend, has delivered on his vision of codifying the principles that have led him to deliver repeated professional services success throughout his career. I look forward to seeing this book's positive impact on the many professional service consultants and organizations around the world.

INTRODUCING THE SEVEN PRINCIPLES

"Principles have no real force except when one is well-fed."

- Mark Twain

A COMMON TALE OF WOE

In 2010, I met a young consultant named Michael Martin. He was a very affable character who was liked by everyone. After graduating in science and engineering, he landed a job as a professional services consultant where he found himself in front of a customer instead of a computer screen. Although he was very capable of deploying his subject matter expertise on his customer's behalf, his ability to recognize and successfully manage critical customer situations was still maturing.

Like millions of other consultants, Michael was proficiently trained as a subject matter expert but at the same time, he was on a challenging journey to evolve himself into a professional who could repeatedly deploy his expertise and generate customer success. This journey from subject matter expert to valuable consultant is slow, dangerous, and imprecise, which ultimately results in varying degrees of success for those who undertake it. If not navigated correctly, this journey can encounter many perilous moments that can prove disastrous for the individual consultant, their customer, and their firm. To illustrate, lets inspect Michael's situation further.

About four years into Michael's career, he achieved a mid-level consultant position as a Solution Architect. This new role came with the responsibility of working directly with the customer and determining how he would help them achieve their goals. In his own words, Michael's will recount his experience as a customer-facing consultant. It perfectly illustrates the risks that all subject matter experts take when they enter the world of delivering that expertise for a fee.

"Early in my professional services career I was put on a project for an enterprise technology company in Silicon Valley. I had recently been promoted to the role of Solution Architect, and this project was one of my first in that new role.

I was more than a little nervous because this was my chance to prove I could create robust technical designs and lead a team of implementation consultants at the enterprise level. The enormous size of this client and the future possibilities for my firm created extra pressure for me to perform well.

From the beginning of the project, I knew that the client had unrealistic expectations that were not compatible with the capabilities of our software. I knew that creating what the customer wanted would require a huge number of customizations, compromises on the client's part, and an excessive number of hours on our part. I also knew it would be massively complex and wholly unmanageable once built. I feared that being too direct in explaining the reality of our circumstances would cause the customer to lose faith in my firm and myself. Even worse, I felt that bringing my concerns to my management team would be an admission of incompetence during my first big chance to prove my value, and I didn't want to blow it!

So the time bomb started ticking. I let the client's expectations stay misaligned. I deferred the need for difficult conversations because I thought if I just worked hard enough I could make the impossible happen. Of course, that's not what happened. The customer's high expectations came crashing down to reality, and ultimately, the project failed. After weeks of executive escalation and bartering, the project could not be saved. Both companies lost a great deal of time and money and my team's manager lost his job. All of this occurred because I was too afraid and too proud to speak up and tackle my customer's misaligned expectations head on.

This experience changed my career, and thankfully, for the better. By analyzing my own actions, I began to understand the value these principles provide. I made a commitment to myself that I would always have difficult conversations, no matter how hard or uncomfortable they were to start. My resolve to avoid repeating this mistake was put to the test almost immediately. On my next engagement, again with an enterprise technology company, I noticed that the client's expectations were not grounded in reality. I spoke up during the engagement kickoff -- our very first meeting. After alerting my management team and the customer to the issues, I then set about helping the customer realign their expectations with what was possible and what would work best for them. In no small part due to the fact I had learned from my mistakes and committed myself to the principles in this book, the project ended up being very successful.

Our team had very high expectations of itself, and I made a mistake. It goes without saying that my firm was very disappointed with the failed outcome, but they also recognized that no one was more disappointed than I. As it had been my first big mistake, they gave me a chance to learn from it instead of punishing me for it. My manager was not as fortunate, but I guess somebody ends up paying a price when something of this magnitude fails. I learned a valuable lesson the hard way, and hence I'm donating my experience in the hope that it can act as a trigger to help you prevent a similar disaster."

Michael's story is unfortunately far too familiar for many of the world's professional services consultants, not to mention the executives that need to step in and deal with the consequences. There is an army of consultants just like Michael who generate the lion's share of a professional services firm's billable hours. I wrote this book primarily because, after witnessing so many examples myself, I began to believe that the problem is more prolific and unaddressed than we sometimes like to admit. Situations like the one Michael faced don't always end in project failure. Instead the engagements are saved at the last minute when the professional services manager or executive capitulates and works for free or for a reduced rate as a way to correct the situation; and most times, it does. While a failed engagement attracts a lot of attention, the revenue that slowly leaks from saved engagements seems to attract much less. They occur so frequently that many services executives treat them as a part of the professional services business. However, my personal experience has led me to believe that not only are these saves an incredibly costly drain on profitability but that a great number of them are entirely avoidable.

Over the years, I have worked hard to turn failing professional services organizations into healthy and successful ones. These situations are so extreme that I must accept that I alone cannot lead the charge on all fronts. To alter the course of failing services organizations, I cannot be bogged down in fixing the plethora of escalations and failing engagements. I must instead break the cycle of escalations by deputizing my team to do this for themselves. This leaves me to focus on repairing the team's core infrastructure such as contracting, pricing, training and quality assurance procedures. This is hard to do if the team as a whole lacks experience to act as efficient deputies. In such situations, I have used and reused a set of principles that have helped me rapidly turn unhealthy services teams into successful engines of growth and customer success.

These principles generate enthusiasm for resolving difficult circumstances quickly, even if that resolution is unpleasant. Rather than resolving every escalation myself, I empowered my team to deal with most of them by applying the same principles I applied. Within a reasonably short amount of time, this principle led approach to remediation begins to work and my team's engagements encounter fewer escalations and we are able to complete them on time and closer to budget. This also results in a much happier portfolio of customers.

The ability for my teams to resolve escalations themselves results in less downtime, as they are not waiting for escalations to be resolved by senior management. This means that engagements complete faster with less non-billable time, which accelerates revenue. Profit margins increase, as there is less time given away for free in order to make the situation right with the customer.

Our management teams also benefit. They have more time available to improve how they are running their businesses because they aren't hindered by the executive escalations that had previously absorbed their time. Reducing escalations also gives our management team the necessary time required to accelerate the turn-around effort. After executing this play a couple of times I realized that when we empowered our consultants to deal directly with these difficult customer interactions, we were simply a more productive professional services organization.

THE NEED FOR BALANCE

I learned long ago that the successful delivery of professional services is all about balance. During my first seven years as a consultant at IBM, I found customers difficult. They were always fun and pleasant to work with, but I found it a challenge to succeed within the engagement's original constraints. Customers kept changing their minds, and I often found that they had unrealistic expectations of the time and funds required to achieve their desired goals. Also, their decision-making took so long that it seemed to always make it difficult to complete the engagement on time.

As the next step in my career, I took an executive position on the other side of the fence and became a consumer of professional services. As a customer, I found that the service providers listened when they wanted to win my business, but soon afterward became more interested in their own plans and budgets than my goals. I often needed to change the objectives we had agreed upon in the contract because my business goals had changed. I was happy to accept responsibility for these changes, but I didn't want to waste time convincing my professional services provider to change with me. The pressures placed upon me by my CEO, our Board of Directors, and our own customers were equal to or greater than any pressure I had known as a service provider. What I needed was a partner that would help me reduce the cost of the necessary change by acting quickly. Having once been in the service provider's shoes, I understood their desire to adhere to the existing plans, but now, my position and perspective had changed. I wanted to work with people to whom I could entrust my goals and know that they would do whatever they could to make me successful, while simultaneously protecting their own profitability.

After a couple of years, I returned to a service provider role with a newfound perspective. My experience on both sides of the fence taught me that I was not as balanced as I needed to be. Sometimes, I leaned too far in the direction of my customer, to the detriment of my employer. At other times, I pushed too hard on behalf of my employer only to aggravate my customer relationship. I determined that if I could find a way to keep a better balance throughout the engagement, my results would surely improve.

To do this, I had to understand more about these recurring conflicts and analyze them from both sides in order to find the right approach to resolving them. I found that there were many different situations in which I needed to strike a specific kind of balance. In the table below, I list the natural tensions that I had noticed. While each set of goals may seem opposing, the reality is that *both* must be satisfied if an engagement is going to be successful.

Customer's Goals		Service Provider's Goals
Achieve my customer's desired business improvements within their time and budget constraints	AND	Achieve the time and profit goals my firm had set for the engagement.
Push hard to keep the engagement progressing	AND	Push hard to stop the engagement if potentially damaging issues arise.
Be fully engaged with my customer's business	AND	Be fully engaged with my own firm and career progression.
Solve customer problems by burying myself in their details	AND	Guide the customer to success by focusing on the bigger picture.

While there are many other situations that can arise during service delivery, it's likely you can identify with some of these challenges. In Michael's opening example, his balance was off. He was unable to recognize the danger and did not take the necessary actions to rebalance accordingly. While customer success is paramount, the reality is that success only occurs when *both* the customer and the service provider achieve their goals. To recognize such a feat you must walk a fine line between your customer's desire to be successful and your firm's ability to deliver an acceptable outcome. This delicate balance has existed as long as people have been delivering complex professional services, and this book will explore the specific principles required to successfully maintain it. The balance required to walk this high wire to success is what I call the *Professional Services Tightrope.*

IT IS A DANGEROUS TIGHTROPE

When you lose your balance, you will fall from the professional services tightrope. In the opening story, Michael fell a considerable distance, but fortunately, he was able to recover from it without any major problems. He was incredibly focused on righting his wrongs and learning from his mistakes. So much so, I hired him again at my next job because I knew what he had been through and how it had changed him for the better.

His direct manager, however, was not so fortunate. He had already suffered sizeable falls, and unfortunately this was another one. Knowing that my own career could only survive a finite number of these falls, I had no alternative but to take action and remove him from the company. The ability for his team to deliver repeatable success was becoming a random event rather than a carefully placed bet.

Failing to instill the principles into his team's service delivery left Michael's manager trying to identify engagement fires across his entire portfolio by himself. If field consultants are not trained in the principles of delivering quality professional services, they are unable to identify the critical moments at which the torch of misalignment is lit under an engagement's straw-like foundation. It will then smolder for a while, and for every minute the manager fails to see the warning signs, the problem worsens. Too many professional services managers and executives pay dearly for their team's failure to identify the smoldering fires that inevitably break into the burning blaze that forces them from their jobs.

As an executive watching many engagements from a distance, it is hard to see the smoke even when you are actively looking for it. Wouldn't it be better for everyone if we simply trained our consultants to spot the smoldering fires? This would be a benefit for the individual consultant, their firm, the customer and the executives in charge.

Professional services executives often recognize that a great consultant brings a level of quality to an engagement. This is because a great consultant is on the lookout for smoke and small fires. When they see or smell a fire, they come running. From experience, I know the increased sense of security that is felt from having my best consultants staffed to an important engagement.

However, over time I have also noticed the peculiar fact that my *best* consultants are not always my *most experienced* ones. This means that, somehow, a small group of younger consultants are able to learn and possess knowledge that more experienced consultants do not. While this may be obvious, it did prompt me to begin thinking about how I could find a way to replicate these all-too-rare phenomena. With such stakes at risk, the gamble of leaving my success to the varying capabilities of field consultants was a game of Russian Roulette that I didn't want to play. There had to be a way to make the odds more favorable.

ACCELERATING A CONSULTANT'S LEARNING CURVE

One day, I walked passed a woman in my team sitting at her desk. I stopped to ask her a question about the engagement she was running when I noticed she had a sticky note on the side of her computer that read "WWSD." After we finished the conversation, I asked her about the note, which resembled an acronym we used at IBM. To my surprise, she responded that it was intended to remind her to think "What Would Shane Do?" As you can imagine, this was a surprise, so I asked her what she meant. She immediately recited many of the common sayings I had repeated for years. She used the sticker as a way to prompt herself to recite the phrases that focused her actions onto the most important issues.

This woman's feedback confirmed that repeating a meaningful phrase could alter a consultant's thought process, and ultimately his or her behavior, in the field. I had been repeating my phrases for years, but I had never deliberately built the ethos of my entire team around them. It became clear that by using phrases that were targeted at achieving positive outcomes, it was possible to communicate the core principles of delivering quality professional services. If I could find a way to simplify and structure these sayings in a meaningful way, I could accelerate the time it takes for a consultant to learn and act the right way.

Since then, I have repeatedly trained professional services consultants by using a specific set of phrases that incorporate the core principles necessary to maintain their balance during an engagement. Each time I have taught these principles, I have found that they have the same positive results in a very short amount of time. I have also received the same feedback from my management teams and former consultants who have progressed their careers and delivered these principles on their own. They are easy to remember and easy to apply to a particular instance. They are also sufficiently descriptive to be acted upon as soon as one recalls them.

These sayings reflect the collective wisdom of our industry's many experienced consultants and executives. I am not the only one who uses many of these phrases, and in fact, I learned many of them from other services executives over time. The aim of this book is to structure a few of these commonly used phrases as a framework that encompasses the fundamental database of professional services knowledge that I believe every consultant must possess.

To achieve such a goal, I had to find a way to arrange them in a way that would provide a concise but meaningful framework. Each principle had to be a call to action while simultaneously providing a broad basis to encapsulate a specific body of knowledge. And, of course, it also had to be easy enough to explain in detail without becoming unwieldy or difficult to comprehend. After many different methods of organizing them, I have settled on the arrangement that I believe works best.

I have termed this final arrangement, "The Seven Principles of Professional Services." As mere words on paper they will not change the way you deliver your service. For that to occur you must adopt the principles as a part of your daily language. This will help you internalize them so they can become integral to the work you do each day. After all, a principle is a belief that is so strong that it begins to shape your thoughts and actions. For that to occur, you must believe in it wholeheartedly. This is hard to do without experiencing the damaging failures that force you to see their necessity. Therefore, the goal of this book is to inspire your faith in them by relating numerous instances in which they've been successfully employed.

The Seven Principles of Professional Services are listed below. To help you understand how each principle relates to your everyday service delivery, I have listed the primary are of focus for each of them.

The 7 Principles of Professional Services	Area of Focus
1. Adapt to Your Environment	Understanding the Customer Environment
2. Always Know What *Done* Looks Like 3. Manage Expectations 4. Have Difficult Conversations Early 5. Think F.A.A.S.T.	Delivering Engagements Successfully
6. Participate in the Collective Wisdom	Optimizing Your Value
7. Stay Engaged	Building a Professional Services Career

These seven principles are central to successfully managing the customer and service provider relationship as well as to successfully managing your professional services career. Whether you have been a consultant for ten minutes or ten years, this book will improve how you think about your customers, and more importantly, the actions you take on their behalf, and on behalf of your firm.

MAINTAINING BALANCE WITH PRINCIPLES

In the world of professional services, you may quickly find that simply being an expert in your chosen field is not enough to achieve repeated success in consulting engagements.

You work in an environment where the customer is always right, where people-to-people relationships are more important than the work itself, and where failing to adhere to deadlines and budgets can provoke your customers to kick you out, or even worse, take legal action! As you already know, your firm's future business (and your reputation) relies on your ability to facilitate your customer's success even in the most trying circumstances.

You may also have identified that a professional service consultant's job is more complicated than just applying your specific skills to the customer's problem. There are a myriad of situations that require something *more* to successfully complete an engagement. To that end, this book's goal is to provide you with the added help you need to keep your balance while you deliver your subject matter expertise. The ability to maintain your balance while utilizing your skills for the customer's benefit is a must when delivering "enterprise-grade" professional services. You cannot be a great subject matter expert *or* a trusted advisor to your customer. You must be both. This book aims to provide you with the added skills you need to confidently walk that tightrope.

The subject matter expertise for which you are paid, account roughly for only 75% of what is required to deliver successful professional services. The remaining skills are those that will help you successfully manage your relationship with your customer and your firm. Like any productive interpersonal relationship, the people involved must build and maintain a level of trust that allows them to work together effectively. To do this successfully, you must have more than subject-matter know-how. You must be a master at managing the ambiguity and nuance of the relationships between you, your firm, and your customer. As your career progresses towards a position in management, you will find that your success will depend more on correctly executing these seven principles than your subject-specific know-how.

If you're frustrated to hear that there's more to learn, don't worry, you're not alone. There are millions of individual professional service consultants just like you, and they are also acquiring these necessary skills through trial and error. The complexity of these skills makes them hard to learn until you have suffered the consequences of not using them correctly. For almost twenty years, I have been considering the complexity of these skills: first from the perspective of a consultant, then from the perspective of a customer, and finally, from the perspective of the executive accountable for delivering success across all fronts. The purpose of this book is to combine and relay the knowledge I've acquired from my own successes and failures. In doing so, I hope to accelerate your ability to achieve your own version of success.

LEARN FROM OTHER PEOPLE'S EXPERIENCES

This book aims to do more than just tell you how professional services executives use these principles. It also aims to inspire your belief in the premise that they can help you improve your own service delivery. By collecting examples from the field that demonstrate the real-life application of the principles, I hope that you can identify the situations in which they apply and begin using them on your own. Michael's opening example is just the first of many that illustrate the impact the principles can have on typical consulting situations. Positive examples reinforce a principle, while more disastrous examples will assist you in realizing the price you may pay for not upholding them.

The key to navigating your path to success is to learn to execute these principles in difficult customer situations. These field examples aim to illustrate each principle's importance, and their results should inspire your belief in them. In turn, I hope that you can recognize their value and begin deploying them yourself in customer-facing situations. In essence, I hope to provide you with the advantage of learning from others mistakes (including mine), rather than having to continue learning from your own. These examples are identified with headings that begin with the words "Field Example:"

WHY GET BETTER AT WALKING THE TIGHTROPE?

It is simply a fact that people like to buy professional services from people they trust. This is because the customer must hire a service provider to deliver a future outcome. The customer must trust that the service provider will make that future outcome possible to the expected level of cost and quality. As a service provider, your ultimate goal is to become the customer's trusted advisor within your field. This trust is earned when you deliver your customer's desired result by successfully walking the professional services tightrope.

If you failed to walk your tightrope successfully, it is unlikely that a customer will work with you again. However, if you have earned the customer's trust, there is a list of benefits that befall you and your firm. These can include the removal of your firm's price as a key decision making criteria during the vendor selection process. It can also mean that you no longer need to compete against other service providers to win that customer's future business. During subsequent engagements with that customer, you will also find that they are more likely to accept your recommendations, as they will trust that you have considered their best interests. This makes subsequent customer engagements simpler, cleaner, and less turbulent, and hence, more profitable! Once you are a trusted advisor, you will find it easier to close new business deals with those customers, which should be the aim of every professional services firm.

In the professional services industry, your future success lies in the degree to which your customers trust you as a business partner. Make your customer successful and you will build a level of trust that your customer will want to rely upon again for similar success. This situation ensures that customers return for more services in the future. While there may be other strategies to generate professional services success, becoming your customer's trusted advisor is always the most lucrative approach!

NOBODY IS PERFECT

Before we begin discussing these principles, it's important to humbly acknowledge our mutual humanity. Nobody is perfect! Even after twenty years of studying, learning, and applying these principles, I still don't adhere to them 100% of the time. And yet, even when I make mistakes, the principles remind me of the areas of my service delivery that require attention. This provides me with actionable follow-up to make sure that I do better next time. For that reason, it is important to manage your expectations of yourself so that when you fail to abide by the principles, your mistakes become a *constructive* learning experience, rather than a *destructive* one.

We are all aware that we should learn from our mistakes. This is certainly true in the world of professional services as you are bound to make many. However, I would advise you to try as hard as you can to learn from other people's mistakes as well. That does not mean that you should revel in someone else's misfortune, but that you should watch carefully when other people make a mistake and observe how your firm corrects it. Regardless of your involvement, every one of these mistakes presents you with a learning opportunity. If you are close enough to witness the fallout from someone else's mistake, then you should make the most of that opportunity to learn how to avoid it yourself in the future. Taking advantage of these learning opportunities will not only provide a personal benefit, but it will also benefit your customers and your firm.

When you fail to apply a principle, there will be a cost, and in our industry, that is simply a part of life. This takes some getting used to. I'm not perfect and neither are you, so don't set yourself up for failure by having unrealistic expectations. Delivering quality professional services is about achieving objective results in a subjective environment. It will never be consistently perfect. The goal of the principles is to act both as a balancing pole to prevent you from falling from the tightrope when you shouldn't, and to act as a safety net to minimize damage when they can, but they are not a fail-safe. In a process that never replicates, the Seven Principles of Professional Services provide you with a framework for obtaining consistent customer success throughout your professional services career.

ADAPT TO YOUR ENVIRONMENT

"Adapt or perish, now as ever, is nature's inexorable imperative."

– H. G. Wells

SUCCESS FROM ADAPTATION

It takes years to learn the technical skills required to walk a tightrope. However, while this accomplishment by itself is incredible, it pales in comparison to the achievement of walking that same rope at extreme heights in an uncontrolled environment in front of a large and noisy crowd. In the dangerous profession of tightrope walking, excellence requires more than just balance. It requires the ability to control one's fear and impulses and to ignore external distractions through immense focus, but at the same time, remaining calm enough to execute the primary skill of maintaining balance. A lapse in this ability could prove fatal. To succeed at such an activity, tightrope walkers must adapt to a perilous environment and faultlessly employ their skills so consistently that the risk of failure becomes minimal enough to consider it a viable career.

Similarly, a professional services consultant performs his or her technical skills in an ever-changing *engagement environment*. It too requires that you remain calm, control your fear, and stay focused in order to achieve success. The engagement environment is established when your professional services firm and the customer agree to do business together. Each agreement results in the creation of a unique environment that requires both parties to work together to achieve mutual success.

One of the core reasons that consultants become frustrated with the consulting profession is that they simply do not fully appreciate the environment in which they are working. As this chapter explains, your customer's business will be alive with activity even prior to your arrival. The events preceding your arrival are significant, and they will have a profound impact on the engagement environment you will encounter. The consultant should be aware of these events and keep an eye out for any telltale signs of their influence. If you fail to understand your engagement environment, you could easily do something that is misinterpreted and make a sensitive matter worse.

Hence, the first principle identifies that you must research the conditions under which the environment was created and adapt as completely as possible to the forces at play within it. Failure to do so will place you at odds with your environment, and your chances of success will diminish significantly.

Even after you have fully adapted to your environment, you must still overcome the challenge of walking your tightrope successfully. The customer must achieve the goals they had set for the engagement, and the service provider must make money and finish the engagement with a satisfied customer. In the same way that a tightrope walker must learn to execute his skills flawlessly in different kinds of environments, you too must learn to adapt to each environment and then execute your skills successfully no matter the conditions.

Despite not having been trained in the importance of understanding the engagement environment, your company has probably sent you into one with an experienced and demanding customer, and now there is a lot riding on your ability to achieve success. Don't despair. Mastering even this one principle will give you insight that you can use to bring clarity to your situation. The more you understand your environment, the greater your chance of adapting to it and succeeding within it. For you, this means simultaneously pleasing your customer and your employer by balancing their respective expectations, even when they appear to be conflicting.

UNDERSTANDING THE ENGAGEMENT ENVIRONMENT

The delivery of professional services is at the tail end of a process that the customer began some time ago. This process starts when one individual decides to commit to improve his or her company's business. This decision, however, does not always lead to the creation of an engagement environment. The engagement environment is only created if the customer employs an external team of experts to provide them with the kinds of services they are unable to obtain from within their own company.

Your professional services firm *is* that team of experts. To survive, your firm must make money from customers looking to improve their business in a subject area in which you have experience and skill. With each engagement, a professional services firm takes a calculated risk that it can provide the requisite people and equipment to deliver the customer's desired improvements for a fee greater than its own cost of supplying those resources.

Yet, despite a number of well-thought calculations by the professional services firm, it never really knows if success is possible because there are so many variables outside of its control. You could say that each engagement represents a gamble by the service provider that they will make the customer happy and make money in the process. The business of professional services *is* a gamble, and just like any professional gambler, a professional services firm knows that it must stack the odds of achieving success in its favor. If the odds cannot be made favorable, the business model is simply too risky to sustain long-term success.

As a professional services consultant, you must understand these origins. By doing so, you provide yourself with every possible chance of understanding the environment's dynamics and working them in your favor. While this may seem self-serving, remember that it is also imperative to your customer that you succeed. A failed engagement will look bad for everyone involved, and the customer would much prefer an active business partner than a reluctant one. Hence, learning how to stack the odds in favor of mutual success is exactly what the customer is paying you to do. To understand the genesis of the engagement environment, lets consider the professional services purchasing process from beginning to end. By doing so, we will cover everything you need to know about the origins of the environment in which you work every day.

Step 1: The Pressure to Improve

Every business is trying to improve its performance by increasing revenues, reducing costs, gaining competitive advantage, or simply finding new customers to sell to. The respective pressures of inflation, competition, and investor expectations all require that a business continue to grow. These businesses are your prospective customers.

Within each of these businesses, there is a select group of people in charge of initiating and delivering business improvements. They are called *Decision Makers*. The decision makers compete against each other for the use of their company's most valuable resources (people and money) by presenting their ideas for improvement to the company's executives. They hope that their ideas will receive approval to be funded. Once funded, the decision maker will enter into the same gamble that drives your professional services firm.

The decision makers are betting that they can achieve an outcome of greater value than the fee they will pay the service provider to help them achieve it. Conversely, if decision makers decide to do nothing and avoid this gamble entirely, they will lose favor (and potentially their jobs) for failing to deliver any improvements. Decision makers also run the risk that their competitors make similar improvements before they do and leap ahead of them in the market. If this happens, it creates a compelling event where the customer has no option but to rapidly improve their business operations or face losing market share. If the decision maker attempts to make an improvement and that effort fails, they stand a good chance of losing their job because valuable company resources will have been wasted.

The number of decision makers within a given company can vary from a small handful to several hundred. Some people enter into a new job position wanting to be a decision maker, while others have it thrust upon them. Almost anyone can become a decision maker. This is why you are likely to encounter a huge spectrum of different personalities when dealing with the people in this role. Each different decision maker has strengths and weaknesses that you will need to deal with.

To be clear, however, it is the owners and shareholders of the company who are demanding that the decision makers find ways to improve the company's performance. They are the people who benefit the most from the company improving its performance, and they employ these decision makers to make sure that it happens. This constant drive for performance improvement is what fuels the customer's need to consume professional services.

Step 2: Justifying the Return – The Business Case

Decision makers will line up to present their ideas to the company executives in order to get their ideas funded. They will present summaries of the expected costs and benefits of their ideas. This summary of business benefits and the costs to achieve them is called a *Business Case*. In addition to outlining why the company needs the improvement, the business case will calculate the financial return that each investment is likely to deliver. This calculation is called the *Return on Investment (ROI)*. It can be measured in money made or saved by the improvement in comparison to the money spent to implement it. It may also be calculated by showing the time (in months or years) it will take for the money spent to be recouped by those additional revenues or savings. The ideas that carry the best ROI are typically the ones that will receive funding.

Once an ROI has been presented, something happens that we must be aware of. An expectation has now been set in the minds of the company executives. If selected, this idea is going to return an improvement of far greater value than the price being paid. Yet, the experts (that's you) haven't had time to complete a thorough evaluation of the effort required to deliver on the commitments that have been made. This situation creates additional risk to the engagement, and it may hamper your chances of success. The degree to which these decisions impact your engagement will vary depending on how thoroughly the decision maker carried out their ROI analysis.

One of the big risks in this situation is that the decision maker may have been very eager to have his or her idea to win the funding competition, and hence, the ROI may be artificially inflated. Remember that companies often choose the ideas with the best ROI, so this creates an environment where underestimating the costs or overstating the benefits of an idea will help the decision maker obtain their funding. Decision makers do not deliberately misrepresent their ROI's, but it happens regularly as a result of several factors such as the desire to win funding, hasty cost and benefit estimation, a lack of detail during the information-gathering process, inexperience, and just plain old human error. If this happens, it will further complicate your experience when it comes time for you to deliver your service.

You must realize that the decision maker always has the option to deliver this business improvement without the help of an external professional services firm. If they have the ability to achieve this improvement by utilizing their own internal people, then acquiring funding is a lot easier, and the process will never engage a professional service firm. However, once the decision maker decides to employ an external team of consultants he or she has a very high expectation that they will engage with experts who are capable of delivering on the promises that have just been made. This means that the customer is now expecting far more of you than they are expecting of their own people because *you* are the expert and you are being paid solely to help them achieve their desired outcome.

The customer is outsourcing all or part of their success to you and they expect you to achieve it exactly as you said you would. This reliance forms the fundamental basics from which almost everything we discuss within this book originates.

Step 3: Acquiring the Funds

Once an idea is approved for funding, the decision maker can now acquire the necessary budget and other resources (such as people) to implement their ideas. The Chief Financial Officer (CFO) is typically the person who provides the money to the decision maker. The CFO is the gatekeeper of all things financial within a company. He or she is in charge of all revenues and expenditures, and, as you can imagine, this is a powerful and high-pressure position. If a company misappropriates money, begins to lose money, or suffers unexpected reductions in profit, the CFO and the Chief Executive Officer (CEO) will be held accountable by the shareholders. Therefore, receiving money from the CFO is a significant event because it places the decision maker in the career "hot seat." If the decision maker can use the money to successfully improve the company's business performance, then his or her chances of promotion and job security will increase. If he or she fails to deliver the promised improvements, the decision maker's job will be at risk.

There are few career-defining moments as significant as acquiring funds from your employer on the promise of providing future improvements. Do it successfully and you will progress upward; fail and you may be looking for a new job.

A great professional services consultant understands the stress this situation creates on those involved. It starts with the CFO appointing the decision maker as the *Executive Sponsor* for the initiative that was funded. This person is now responsible for using those funds to return the benefits promised to the company executives. To make this happen, the executive sponsor will assemble an internal team to assist the service provider in implementing the expected improvements within the assigned time and budget. In doing so, this internal team of customer employees is also in the "hot seat" and must deliver the benefits that the decision maker has promised. As you can see, there are now several careers on the line, and they will all feel the pressure of having to make the engagement successful. The way your customer's organization applies pressure will impact the environment you will encounter during the engagement. You must take the time understand this environment and its surrounding culture, and you must be prepared to handle the situations it creates.

Step 4: Vendor Selection – Request for Proposal (RFP)

Anybody selling anything to a customer is considered a *vendor*. To your customers, you are a vendor. To select the right professional services vendor, the customer is likely to employ a process where different vendors' prices and capabilities are pitted against each other in the hope of identifying the one that is most likely to make them successful. This process is called *Vendor Selection*. The goal of this process is to ensure that the company's funds are spent on the vendor that is most likely to bring about success. Spending the allocated funds and not achieving success is a failure that no executive sponsor wants to explain to their CFO.

This process begins when the customer requests that you and your competitors submit a proposal (a formal version of which is called a Request for Proposal or RFP). This request provides your firm with an idea (in summary or in detail) of the required outcomes. In sending the RFP to your firm, the customer is inviting you to provide a solution that will help them achieve their desired result. They will also ask that you detail the timeline and budget required for them to purchase these services from you. In some companies, this step is where the professional services team begins its interaction with the customer. In some organizations there are a small number of experienced consultants who are assigned on a part-time or full-time basis to answer RFP's.

Regardless of who is responsible, someone in your firm will respond to the customer's request with a proposal indicating the likely cost, timeline, and benefit to the potential customer. Creating a proposal like this involves listening to the customer's requirements, gathering as much information as possible about the customer's environment, and then determining the level of time and effort required to deliver the customer's desired outcomes. This initial round of responses from the vendors is the first external account of the expected time, effort, and money required to successfully achieve the customer's desired results. This is a very critical stage in the process, and its importance should not be overlooked. Up until this point, the customer's expectation about the time, effort, and price required to achieve success has come solely from internal experts not sufficiently qualified to do the job themselves. Hence there is a good chance that the vendors estimates to achieve success are outside of the customer's original budget.

In many circumstances, the customer closely guards the preliminary ROI calculations used to determine the funding budget. This is typically done in the hope that the service providers will quote a lower price than the amount being funded, but the reality is that the quotes typically exceed it. This happens because the non-experts who developed the business case traditionally overlook the requisite smaller details required for a successful outcome. They tend to underestimate the effort required to achieve complex outcomes with quality. This includes, but is not limited to, the depth of technical detail required, the complexity of thorough testing activities and project management overhead.

When this happens, it puts the decision maker under immediate pressure. He or she will not want to go back to the CFO to ask for more money at such an early stage in the engagement. Hence, the decision maker will attempt to convince the service provider to reduce their prices to be within the required budget. This begins the process of commercial negotiation, which is intended to bring the service provider's prices within the allocated budget.

It is possible however, for the whole vendor selection process to be simplified and the need for competitive bidding to be removed. This exception occurs when a specific service provider has an existing and close relationship with the executive sponsor (or other senior customer executive). In this scenario, the service provider is automatically selected because of their *trusted advisor* status. In such cases, the executive sponsor will contact that service provider and say, "I need your people." While price may still be negotiated, the service provider's price is no longer compared to a list of competitors. This preserves higher margins by not having to reduce the price to win the business. Don't you want to be that service provider? Of course you do, but so does every other service provider. This scenario can only occur if you have previously made this customer successful and earned their ongoing trust.

Step 5: Vendor Selection – Commercial Negotiation

In the event that multiple service providers are still bidding for the customer's work, the customer will begin to consider the different proposals they receive. They will compare them against each other in an attempt to identify the one that will provide them the best solution for the best price. During this process, both the service provider's scope of work and their estimated price are heavily scrutinized. This begins the commercial negotiation of the price, time, and effort provided by the vendors. It is aimed at making sure that the customer receives the greatest business benefit possible for the best possible price. This does not mean that the lowest price always wins. However, price is often the primary decision criteria in purchases such as these, as money is the rarest of all company resources, and the quality of unknown service providers is very difficult to evaluate reliably.

In a competitive price situation many service providers continue to cut their price and effort estimates in a desperate endeavor to keep revenue flowing into the business. They would rather bid a low deal than get no deal. This willingness to accept underestimated prices can create an environment where the engagement's core expectations (price, effort, time, and quality) can easily become severely misaligned for the following reasons:

> **Reason 1:** The executive sponsor is being paid to not waste company resources and like all good buyers, wants the most value for the least cost. This means that he or she will continue to push for price discounts until the service provider gives them a best and final offer. Added to this, the executive sponsor's original funding estimate may have been ill-informed, and hence, he or she will continue to push the service provider to reduce their proposal's price until it fits within that budget.

> **Reason 2:** Your salesperson is competing against other companies salespeople whom are all positing their services as superior, faster, cheaper, and of better quality than yours. Given that your salesperson is only paid if they win the deal, it is easy to see how scope, time, price, and quality can become overly optimistic during this negotiation. Your salesperson needs to close deals to

survive, so they may exhibit a willingness to shave dollars off the price, or underestimate the weeks necessary for completing the timeline. To a commission-based salesperson and their managers, these actions are often needed to close the sale.

Reason 3: Your firm may simply need the work. Some firms may take the decision that a badly priced deal is better than no deal at all. It is easy for me to say that a service provider should walk away from poorly estimated deals, but the reality is that only the most established of firms are able to take such an approach. If you are an executive of a professional services firm that has a low utilization rate and a quarterly revenue target to achieve, then even a desperately underpriced and over-committed deal may look better than letting the situation get worse.

Although the *vendor selection process* is typically run well, this process is fraught with possible miscommunications and misunderstanding. In extreme cases, the high expectations of the ill-informed customer meet with the desires of the overeager salesperson employed by a revenue-starved service provider. *This is a dangerous combination.*

The danger arises from the fact that your firm may have agreed to revise the original estimate several times in order to win the business. I like to call this revised and deal-winning estimate a *"yestimate"* because it is an estimate that has the primary purpose of making the customer say, "Yes, we will buy your services." This process of re-estimation usually takes place during a period of high activity where the engagement's estimate is changed rapidly many times in order to find the precise *"yestimate"* that will win the business.

In such an environment, it is very common that the alterations made to the engagement's scope and price were not clearly articulated to the customer by the service provider. Even if they were, the customer rarely comprehends them as they are working with many service providers offering different proposals. Hence, there is a strong possibility that some kind of misalignment has already occurred between the service provider's winning proposal and the customer's expected benefits. If this has occurred then the engagement is already misaligned before it begins.

The description of this process is not intended to cause despair or to suggest that the customer, your firm, or the sales representatives are doing anything wrong. They're simply doing their respective jobs, and this is the best available process in our industry for selecting vendors. Until someone invents a better one, this process is simply a part of doing business. Not every engagement contract is won with these worst-case scenario circumstances, and in fact, if this were the norm, then professional services as a business would cease to be profitable. That said however, you can almost guarantee that in a competitive bid for complex professional services, that some kind of misalignment has already occurred. I have detailed this process thoroughly so that you can understand the initial activities that formed your engagement environment in the hope that you can understand how these misalignments may have been created.

To whatever degree possible, you should avoid letting these circumstances upset you. You are not in a position to change this process, and you'll have to learn to deal with the scenarios it creates. If you're going to succeed as a service provider, you must accept the shortcomings of the process and learn to succeed in spite of them. Your career is depending on your ability to deliver services with pinpoint precision amidst an environment fraught with ambiguity. Hence, it is unproductive and pointless to allow the process to frustrate you. More importantly, you must *adapt to your environment.*

The *vendor selection process* concludes with the customer and the vendor negotiating the contractual terms upon which they both agree. This process is called *Contract Negotiation.* You will seldom be intimately involved with this process, so I will spare you too many of its details. For now let's leave this process to senior management and assume that the process is completed without your further involvement. That said, you should always be aware that this process could still further alter your engagement's scope, budget, and timeframe. Hence it is a best practice for you to review the contract prior to the engagement's kick off.

Once the contract is signed, the two organizations have legally agreed that the vendor will provide services aimed at achieving a specific business outcome, in exchange for a fee that the customer agrees is acceptable. In other words, the customer and the service provider are bound by law to maintain their relationship until they mutually agree that their respective objectives have been met. Hence, the contract becomes the engagement's most important document as it provides the legal conditions under which the engagement environment is both created and ended.

Step 6: The Engagement Kick Off

Now that you have contracted to provide your professional services, your customer and your firm combine to create a new and unique engagement environment. Both you and the customer have now taken respective bets that a successful outcome can be achieved within this new environment. The first dawn of this new engagement environment is likely to be heralded by a meeting called the Engagement Kick Off. This meeting is the first chance for the services team and customer to align their expectations of the engagement's purpose and anticipated outcomes. You should anticipate that this meeting will uncover *some* misalignment. This is just one of many situations that require you to develop the skills and techniques covered in this book. While you are the expert on the customer's selected subject matter, you must also be the expert in handling the tricky situation of misaligned expectations. With the help of this book, you will be able to identify these situations as a chance to earn your customer's trust.

If you find misaligned expectations during this meeting and take actions to correct them immediately, you will make great strides towards earning your customer's trust, and you'll also improve your chances of success. If you do not, the engagement begins on an unstable foundation, and you will almost certainly have to go through a costly realignment later. A great professional services consultant will ensure that any misaligned expectations are identified and addressed during the kick off process. This will help prevent future escalations and increase the engagement's chances of a successful outcome.

Step 7: The Engagement

Your employer is likely to have a prescribed way of implementing its services. While this book is not about the value of differing engagement methodologies, I must state that all professional services consultants should follow the delivery processes prescribed by their firm.

The best practices and processes prescribed by your firm are a crucial roadmap to success. Failing to follow them will only hamper your engagement and your career progression. You should demonstrate your value by using, and when necessary, improving the existing processes rather than circumventing them.

This does not mean that freethinking and creative solutions are not a part of your job description. There is no perfect methodology, and no one can accurately predict the entire gamut of customer variations you may encounter. To achieve success in these situations, you will always need to think on your feet. The key to success is to become an expert on your firm's recommended process so that you can creatively bend it (without breaking it) to solve unexpected problems as they arise. Likewise, if you are going to break new ground and discover new ways of achieving success, you must first learn and perfect the existing knowledge. That way you can understand the consequences of your new ideas, and you are more able to accurately predict their chances of success.

More importantly, as a member of a professional services team, you should never deviate from the prescribed method unless you have specific permission from the appropriate authority within your firm. If something goes wrong as a result of your failure to follow the process, you're faced with a bad situation. You have ignored the best practices prescribed to you, and you have failed to deliver customer success. This makes you the person to blame. If the process failed you, or you misinterpreted the process, then you have a way of saving yourself. If you blatantly circumvented the processes, then you are unlikely to build trust with either your customer or your firm. In addition, the customer may use your failure to follow a prescribed process as a reason for them not to pay for the services they received from you. This further compounds your problem as not only do you have an escalation that requires your firm's attention, but you may also have a payment dispute that could result in your firm losing money.

Remember, it is your job is to follow your employer's guidelines to achieve a successful outcome. If you're finding it difficult to succeed within those guidelines, you should discuss the matter with your manager and review alternative approaches.

Step 8: Concluding the Engagement

Concluding an engagement can often be difficult. Many days or months have passed since the customer asked you to deliver what they *believed* they wanted. It is common for customers to change their minds on certain elements of an engagement as it draws to an end. Don't perceive this as indecision, and don't be annoyed by it. This uncertainty is perfectly understandable.

As you have learned, the customer's team is under a lot of pressure, and now that the engagement is nearing its finish, the pressure will naturally intensify as the company's executives begin to anticipate the performance improvements the engagement has promised to deliver. Your customer's team will begin to feel as though every little detail must be right and, hence, they may surprise you by demanding last minute changes. As the engagement concludes, they will likely have spent or exceeded their allocated funds. These budget constraints may prompt heated conversations. During this time of heightened tension, it is incumbent upon the professional services consultant to understand the situation and remain calm and constructive.

If it begins to look as though the outcomes you are providing are not aligned with the outcomes your customer is expecting, then your customer's stress-levels will increase even further. When their stress builds, different individuals will behave differently. Some people may behave erratically, or they may become terse, even to the point of yelling or cursing. Be prepared to handle this situation, and focus your team on resolving the issue rather than assigning blame. A significant part of this book is dedicated to helping you either avoid bad situations or to employ techniques that will aid you in successfully managing them.

As a professional services consultant, you must anticipate this increased tension. At this critical juncture, your reaction will determine whether the engagement concludes swiftly and successfully, or whether it drifts aimlessly. At this point, your customer is depending on you to provide two specific areas of focus:

Focus 1: To provide a clear vision of the plan to complete the engagement (we will refer to this later as knowing what "done" looks like). We will discuss later how easy it is for the big picture goals of an engagement to get lost in the ever-changing details.

Focus 2: To ensure that the vision to complete the engagement aligns perfectly with the agreed contract. You cannot complete the conditions of the contract if you have agreed to a vision that is different from it.

When handled correctly, the engagement environment is concluded upon successful completion of the engagement's original objectives. When handled incorrectly, the engagement environment can turn nasty, and it can be filled with many turbulent events. It is important to recognize that no matter how turbulent the storm, the role of the consultant is to master the conditions and successfully walk the professional services tightrope.

To achieve a successful outcome, you must be determined. It takes an incredible amount of balance to walk the tightrope in this environment. On one hand, the customer will continue to throw changes at you, and you feel committed to satisfying them. On the other hand, you must maintain your firm's profitability, and you are not authorized to accept those changes. Like the tightrope walker, you've got to strike the right balance.

Step 9: Earning Repeat Business

Step 9 is probably the reason you were willing to endure so much in steps 4 through 8. If you have successfully executed the engagement, you may have done it well enough to earn the customer's trust as an advisor in these matters. This is good news because the customer may begin to consider you for repeat business. Repeat business is when the same customer asks you back to perform more work because they were so delighted with the first engagement's outcomes. No matter how precisely a professional services team runs their implementation model, subsequent engagements environments are almost always calmer and more effective environments to work in. These environments tend to provide professional services firms with opportunities that are not only easier to win, but also yield a better customer result and a higher profit margin for the service provider. The following table will help you to understand why this happens and why it is so important that you set your sights on earning this kind of business.

WHEN WINNING NEW BUSINESS...	WHEN WINNING REPEAT BUSINESS...	THE REPEAT BUSINESS ADVANTAGES...
The customer environment is unknown so there is a higher chance that you will uncover unexpected issues.	The customer environment is known so you are less likely to uncover unexpected issues.	• More accurate decisions about how to achieve successful outcomes environment. • Fewer issues are encountered.
The customer is managing you to your contract commitments.	The customer is more flexible with respect to the contract.	• The customer trusts that you are providing value for money. Hence your pricing is not compared to competitors.
There is no prior experience on which to base your estimates and recommendations.	Previous experience helps you provide better estimates and recommendations.	• You are more likely to accurately estimate the effort and price required to be successful • Less trial and error to find the right answers for the customer.
The customer is likely to open the opportunity up to your competitors.	The customer is likely to open the opportunity exclusively to you.	• Better profit margins mean that your company can continue to invest in hiring new people or acquiring better resources. This growth is critical to your success in front of the customer and your desire to want to stay with your employer.
Price is a key decision criterion.	Trust and the likelihood of success become the deciding factors and price becomes less important.	

As you can see, *repeat business* creates an engagement environment that is much better to work in. It is simply easier to win and is also more likely to be successful for both the customer and the service provider with less escalation and agitation. In all of the professional services organizations I have worked, the first customer engagements have carried higher risk and tighter profit margins than subsequent engagements. After a successful initial engagement, subsequent business is less scrutinized, the customer is more aligned as a partner, and they are more willing to pay for the same people who had previously made them successful. Unless there is a reason to restrict your company to new business only (which some fast growing companies may do), repeat business is the easiest and most profitable way to operate a professional services business.

Summary: Understanding the Engagement Environment

As you can see, you didn't land this engagement by chance, and the fact that your customer has high expectations of you is not just because they are demanding. These expectations are simply inherent to the engagement environment. Each engagement is unique and, hence, you must walk your tightrope differently if you want to succeed within it. While each engagement requires effort to achieve success, it is almost always easier to achieve it in an environment created by a customer with whom you have had previous success. Without question, many companies make money on first engagements, so it can be a successful business model. However, the sweeter pot is always the easier and more profitable *repeat* business environments. Once you begin to earn repeat business, you can start to earn your status as the customer's trusted advisor because the environments you create together are considered safe and more likely to yield successful outcomes. As I have stated, this should be every professional services firm's priority.

THE BASIC DYNAMICS OF AN ENGAGEMENT ENVIRONMENT

Now that you understand how an engagement environment starts and ends, lets look at the basic dynamics that are at play while it exists. These environmental dynamics are created as a result of the process we have just covered. The customer is gambling that the service provider understands their vision of success adequately, and can deliver it for a price that was agreed under fierce competition. The service provider is gambling that they can satisfy the customer's need for the price they have agreed, and can negotiate extra funds to cover any part of that vision they may have missed or misunderstood.

While we will discuss more complex dynamics as we walk through the principles, this basic premise of two parties taking rather large gambles on each other creates a small but important list of dynamics that you must be aware of. By understanding and using them to your advantage, you stack the odds of mutual success in your favor.

You Are the Hired Gun

As we have just described, your customers are gambling their future careers on your ability to make them successful. This creates the engagement environment's two most important dynamics.

The first dynamic is that the customer expects you to be the expert. They expect you to not make mistakes. They can sometimes expect you to know far more than you actually do. You must learn to take all of this in your stride and deal with these situations in a calm and constructive manner. This dynamic exists because it is the customer that is paying for your time. They are the buyer and within reason, they have every right to demand the success you committed to provide as a part of your proposal. In their minds, you exist solely to make them successful, and for the most part, that is exactly what you should aim to do.

The second dynamic, is that you have the ability to prescribe a solution to the customer even when they may tell you that they want something different. When an expert speaks, people listen. Within limits, a poor decision by the customer can be corrected by the service provider's wealth of knowledge within their given area of expertise. I have seen too many engagements fail because service providers did not use this dynamic to correct a failing engagement's direction. The reason this happens is because we sometimes like to believe the old adage that "the customer is always right". At a macro level this is true. However, at ground level, where your services are delivered, your customer's team is betting their careers that you will correct them when they are wrong.

Remember, to do no harm. Your customer is the engagement's ultimate authority and that cannot be forgotten. They can pull an engagement out from under you at a moments notice, so never force a customer against their will. If you have to resort to this kind of measure to change a customer's mind then you are not acting as a trusted advisor. True success is going to rely on your ability to identify the moments to emphasize your expert status and when to back down and listen to the customer's advice. You are the expert at what you do; the customer is an expert at what they do. Success only comes when you combine your strengths equally.

Most Customers Are Perfectly Reasonable

Most of the people you meet at a customer site are just like you. They are trying to earn a living and forge a career from which they and their families can benefit. It is rare that you will encounter an entirely unreasonable customer. These people are however under a lot of pressure. They are being paid to achieve the greatest possible outcome within the budget they have been allocated, and this pressure is often transferred directly to you.

The person sitting across the table, who is refusing to sign the change order you just proposed, could be doing so for many reasons. The least likely of which is that they truly want you to fail. For this reason, you must make the effort to see through this façade and connect with the reasonable personality that is sitting behind it. Despite what a lot of people say, customers generally do not expect professional services for free unless the service provider has acted with clear negligence. Most customers will agree to pay a fair price for a fair days work. They will also not pay full price for work done poorly. This is perfectly reasonable. Even in the most difficult of engagement situations, if you can act with a calm and constructive demeanor, and your customer can do the same, the two of you will resolve the issue to your mutual satisfactions.

Calmer Heads Usually Prevail

Do not get drawn into overly emotional disagreements and don't let emotional pleas force you into an action you know is ill advised. Your job is not to inflame a difficult situation, but to find a path forward. This can only happen if you remain calm and constructive. I will repeat the words "calm and constructive" many times throughout this book. This deliberate repetition is attempting to embed the term in your mind in the hope you will remember it when needed.

If you are in a difficult and heated situation, take solace in the fact that, calmer heads usually prevail. People do not stay angry at each other for very long. After a heated disagreement, they learn to put any harsh and untrue words aside and just deal with the problem at hand. As we have just discussed, most of the people you are going to work with are perfectly reasonable people and for the most part, they will not let anger, disappointment, or fear affect the outcome of an engagement.

Use the Hierarchy

Engagements, just like any structured organization, have well defined hierarchies. A hierarchy empowers the more experienced people to preside over the most important decisions about how to operate successfully. Both you and your customer have an engagement hierarchy. Hence, you should be aware that sometimes it is not *what* is said, but *who* says it that has the greatest impact. For this reason, do not be afraid to utilize the hierarchy for full effect. If there is an important decision to be made, and the customer's team is not listening to you, discuss this with your immediate superior and identify if having him or her say it will have a greater effect.

I often find that engagements become totally misaligned because a consultant allows the customer to override his or her decision but does not escalate the situation to an immediate manager. If you truly believe that something has occurred that will put the engagement at risk then you must raise it with your manager and see if they have the ability to alter the outcome. I have often found when done correctly, a simple email or phone call from one executive to another can reverse a poor customer decision. This is a very important dynamic that you must learn to work in your favor.

Beware of "All Care and No Responsibility"

The phrase *"All care and no responsibility,"* is often said about people who have strong opinions about an issue, but who are ultimately not responsible for the quality of how that issue gets resolved. These people can be very dangerous, as they may insist on resolving an issue in a manner that is not consistent with the engagements objectives.

The people who are responsible for the outcome of an engagement are those that understand that both teams are up on a high wire. They know that there are contractual constraints (such as time, budget and planned effort) that must be adhered to. If these constraints are ignored and pushed too hard, there will be consequences. People who are not accountable for the outcomes of the engagement do not understand the need for balance and do not suffer the consequences of falling. Hence, they will continue to push for what they want, or what they believe are the best outcomes for themselves.

The effect of such people on an engagement environment can be disastrous. They will slowly drag the engagement off course. Then when the detour is finally recognized, the people responsible for the engagement will be furious that you listened to their direction. Hence, you must identify which people in the engagement environment are truly responsible for it. These are the people that you should listen to the most because they have a lot invested in obtaining success within the engagements contractual constraints. While you should listen to everyone courteously, do not get distracted by people who are trying to win big but have no stake in the game. Always check with those who are truly responsible for the engagement's success, and confirm that a specific person has the authority to divert or redirect your work.

Quality Versus Time

During all engagements there is a constant battle between the level of quality to which an outcome can be delivered, and the time it takes to achieve that quality. You will often have to decide if you should take more time to complete an activity to a higher level of quality, or deliver it to the customer (or to your own team), "as is" to meet the deadline.

While there is no right answer to this conundrum, I do prefer the following approach.

In almost all circumstances, it is better to be late and of higher quality, than to be on time and of lesser quality. While I am sure that there are exceptions to this approach, I find the pressure created to meet deadlines pales into the long-term significance of providing a quality outcome. I am fairly confident in saying that customers remember the quality of your work, far longer than they remember a small time delay. You should discuss this conundrum with your manager when it occurs. When you consume more time for a task, there are other consequences (such as cost), but simply being aware of this dynamic and managing it with eyes wide open will serve you well.

ADAPTING TO THE ENGAGEMENT ENVIRONMENT

Early in my career at IBM, I became frustrated by the unreasonable demands of customers. I never had a problem with standing my ground in these situations, but I was frustrated because I didn't understand why these escalations happened so frequently. Upon some internal reflection, I started to see myself as the common thread across these situations, and I began to wonder if *I* was problem? However, the more I talked about these issues with other professional services consultants, the more I realized that nearly all of them had similar experiences, and that their customers shared these same traits. Some even had far worse stories than mine!

I was beginning to realize that, although the business objectives differed among customers, the patterns of human interaction across them all seemed to be the same. The process of asking someone else to make or break your career was both necessary and terrifying for our customers. In each situation, the customer had promised to achieve something that they were not able to achieve by themself. Hence, they had to enlist us to help them achieve it. Realizing that my customer was outsourcing their future success to me turned my frustration into empathy. It also opened my eyes to the fact that I was wasting time trying to fight against the environment around me. There was nothing I could do to change the pressures being applied to my customers. If I was going to be successful in such an environment, I had to accept the conditions it presented and learn to navigate through them rather than fight against them.

I was beginning to realize that my customers wanted a business partner who understood their environment and was capable of identifying the best means of achieving success within it. I started to believe that if I knew more about the customer's business, then I could be more able to guide all of us to success. This meant that I had to speak their language. I had to identify with their pains and have the same urgency to resolve them as if I were feeling their pain directly. If I could do this, then I would also demonstrate myself as a trusted advisor.

During my next engagement, I studied my customer's business in depth. They were a state-run Department of Transportation, and I was delivering an engagement in the roads maintenance division. I set about learning the nuances of planning, funding, building and maintaining road segments. More importantly, I talked to the government employees and contractors about their jobs. I understood their roles and how they earned them. I understood what they liked about their jobs, as well as what they hated. In doing so, I began to understand how to use my skills to help them achieve their goals. The result was a far more successful and less frustrating engagement and mutual success was achieved.

Because of the connections I had made with the customer's team, they invited me back to work on numerous other initiatives. They didn't care how much IBM charged them for my time. I was valued as one of their most productive team members. A customer stakeholder who identifies a vendor that can make him or her successful will always look for opportunities to keep using that vendor! Hence, if you want your customers to return to you, you must learn how to facilitate their success first, and then consider how to position that success so that you can also achieve your own.

The constant focus required to attain this level of customer success reminds me of the classic scene from the movie *Glengarry Glenross*, where Alec Baldwin admonishes his sales team by demanding that they follow the principle of "ABC," "Always Be Closing." In a scene that proves humorous to anyone who has worked in a sales environment, he venomously berates the sales team to the brink of breaking them. His character is trying to make the point that no man present in the room is fit to call himself a salesman unless he is constantly pushing the customer towards the closure of a deal. While I have no venom in stating this to you, I echo the exuberance and passion of Alec Baldwin's character in reminding you that a good consultant must similarly follow their own version of "ABC"-- *"Always Be Consulting!"* To abide by this, you must adopt the following habits.

- Ask questions

- Be engaged with their business

- Constructive recommendations

Ask Questions

Typically, service providers become laser-focused on the problems they are hired to solve. This trait is necessary in delivering customer success; however, as we have discussed, the trusted advisor's long-term value only becomes apparent to the customer if the initial engagement is successful. To maximize his or her long-term value during the initial engagement, the professional services consultant should continually absorb and understand the customer's business, not just the problem at hand. In so doing, the consultant demonstrates true value to the customer, and hence, becomes an indispensible part of the customer's ongoing success.

The customer may not always offer lots of information, nor will they initially volunteer more detail than you ask for. Prior to you becoming a trusted advisor, the customer may even be guarded in responding to questions. However, over time, the relationship will strengthen, and the customer will become more open about their business. They may even share strategic initiatives, intercompany obstacles, or specific business challenges, all of which could introduce you to opportunities for repeat business.

A great professional services consultant will ask questions like this:

- How do you think the outcomes from our current engagement will help your day-to-day job?

- Can you help me understand the relationship between what we are doing here and this other part of your business?

- What are the biggest obstacles you think you will need to tackle in the next 12 months?

- Your division seems to be doing well, how is the rest of the company doing?

- Is there anything urgent looming on your company's horizon?

- Is there anything else we could be doing for you?

Any question that asks the customer to open up about their business is an excellent opportunity for you to gain insight and build valuable trust. In the beginning, be prepared for short answers that do not divulge too much information, but eventually more information will flow and you can begin to use it to demonstrate value beyond your present engagement.

Upon asking questions, it is equally important to listen to their answers. I have often seen consultants ask a lot of questions and then ignore the direction and insight their customer's answers provide. You have not worked in the same environment as your customer as long as they have, so processing their answers with their lens can be difficult. While it's important to actively listen to your customer's answers, you should also place yourself in their shoes. You should try to think as if you were working in that environment and understand how it might feel if the same pressures were being applied to you. Without doing this, the answers to your questions are not providing you with the value they could be.

Be Engaged with Their Business

To be effective, a professional services consultant must understand the customer's business model. Although business models tend to repeat themselves across different industries, it is important to understand the specifics of each industry you are working within including the typical metrics by which success is measured. For example, if you are working with a wireless phone company, you should know that it is a high volume low margin business, which requires high capital cost to create a network that can be used by millions of subscribers. It may also be beneficial for you to know that the industry has a key metric called ARPU (Average Revenue Per User), which is calculated and compared against another key metric called the "churn rate" (the rate at which customers are leaving). All wireless phone companies want the ARPU to go up while also trending churn rates down.

Even this basic knowledge is readily available on the internet, so finding it shouldn't be an issue. Company results, analyst's calls, and industry white papers are usually available for any one to access, not to mention that every industry has a myriad of sites that publish relevant articles from which you can learn a great deal. I guarantee that within an hour of researching almost any industry, you will begin to discover ways in which your knowledge could assist a customer within it. Even basic information will give you an ability to open up meaningful discussions with your customer. Don't be afraid to ask customers to clarify when industry specific jargon is used. Even this level of interest is appreciated. Once acquired, this knowledge can help you connect the dots between your customer's business drivers and the services you provide. This is extremely valuable for identifying new ways that your skills can assist the customer and acquiring new business. This is a critical characteristic of a successful professional services consultant.

Finally, it is also extremely important to know the customer's position within their marketplace. Are they the industry leader trying to surge ahead? Are they an acquisition target? Are they trying to broaden their reach or diversify into different markets? Publicly traded companies often have this kind of information recorded in their readily available quarterly reports. This information can drastically change how you approach a specific business challenge and propose possible solutions. It also helps you narrow in on conversation topics that are important to your customer. The more they talk to you, the more they will trust you. This is going to make it easier for you to help them and coincidentally it may also provide you with a chance to identify additional future business.

Constructive Recommendations

Once you have a clear idea of future opportunities, you must sufficiently understand your own firm's capabilities to determine whether it's worth chasing the opportunity. There is no point chasing an opportunity that your company can't fulfill. I have frequently met with consultants who have a great idea about how to answer a specific customer challenge, but the proposed solution is so misaligned with our own business model that it would prove little more than an unprofitable distraction to try and resolve it for just one customer. Although well intentioned, the consultant's ideas neglect to evaluate whether we could succeed at such an endeavor. Nevertheless, these ideas are also a source of innovation, and they inspire us to pursue new services. To ensure your ideas get a fair hearing, consider your firm's ability to provide such a service before raising it to your manager. It is also critical to consider whether or not your idea only applies to a handful of your customers, or whether it applies to a majority of them. The latter is always an idea that your firm should be considering.

Summary: Adapting to the Engagement Environment

To earn your customer's respect, you must learn about their day-to-day challenges. When a professional services consultant commits to learning how an industry operates, the customer will surely take notice. Knowing your customer's business environment will make it easier for you to identify opportunities for them, some of which may require additional services from you. Over time, you may even find that it is *your* ideas that begin the whole business improvement process.

Don't underestimate the value of making your customer look successful within their business environment. By adapting yourself to your customer's environment, you can establish yourself as a critical part of their future success. In doing so, you can lock yourself (and your firm) into a long-term and profitable relationship with your customer.

"Always Be Consulting" is about applying three simple techniques to your everyday routine. Once you've demonstrated that you understand your customer's problems and that you share a similar level of urgency in trying to fix them, you can begin to make accurate decisions on their behalf. This is how you build trust. Once you have earned their trust, both of you can walk your respective tightropes a little easier. Your mutual footing will be more stable because you will be supporting each other across the wire.

CHAPTER SUMMARY

When a customer decides to make a business improvement that requires expert assistance, it creates the engagement environment. You will work in this environment each and every day when delivering your services. If this environment is not navigated correctly, it can significantly damage your chances of success. In order to deliver a quality service and achieve successful customer outcomes, you must understand your engagement environment and adapt to the conditions within it. A part of that adaptation is to learn as much as you can about your customer's business, which means more than just understanding the goals of your current engagement.

In my opinion, our industry's understanding of this principle is weak and seldom properly applied. Unless you are trained by one of the large systems integrators, it is unlikely that the environments in which you operate are given this degree of consideration. However, merely grasping the concepts outlined in this chapter will aid you in this endeavor and can assist you in making more effective decisions. Once mastered, this principle provides a solid step forward in your ability to become a seasoned professional services consultant.

If you are not practicing this principle already, then you should be. Just like a performer walking a tightrope, you cannot begin your endeavor without first understanding the environment in which you will need to cross that wire. Once those skills have been acquired you can begin to focus on furthering your skills up on the wire. If your environment is constantly distracting you, then you cannot focus on letting your technical skills shine through. Failure to adapt to your environment can lead to situations that will throw you off balance and make walking the professional services tightrope far more difficult than it need be.

ALWAYS KNOW WHAT *DONE* LOOKS LIKE

"Where there is no vision, the people perish."

– Proverbs 29:18

VISUALIZING THE OUTCOME

People who walk tightropes (or perform any dangerous feat) emphasize the importance of visualizing a successful outcome at all times. This crystal clear focus on the final outcome helps the performer remain 100% focused on getting across the wire, ensuring that unimportant matters do not become a distraction. Once you've walked out onto that wire, there is no mid-point exit, and there is no turning back. The situation demands the highest level of concentration, and it requires the performer to focus clearly and intently on reaching the other end of the wire.

Similarly, the only way for a professional services engagement to succeed is for you and your customer to reach the end of the engagement without succumbing to the pressures of the environment around you. Whether it is getting to the other side of a tightrope or finishing an engagement, we define the final state in which we visualize the conclusion of our journey as *being done*. The principle of always knowing what *done* looks like requires that *everyone* (both the service provider and customer teams) understands the mutually-agreed criteria that will determine the engagement's successful conclusion. If there is not a common definition of *done*, then individual team members from both parties will all be heading towards different versions of *done,* and the engagement cannot end successfully.

Within an engagement environment, you can think of *done* as being the exact location at which you and your customer will meet after travelling there by different routes. Without well-defined directions and a detailed description of the place you are looking for, you or the customer may arrive at different places. This may mean that part of journey (or even the entirety of it) was a waste of time and effort. For this reason, every member of both the service provider's and customer's teams must be visualizing the same exact place at which they wish to finish their journey. This is the only way for both teams to arrive there safely. This singular vision of the engagement's outcome is what *done* looks like.

The criteria by which *done* is measured is often called the *Engagement Acceptance Criteria,* and these criteria outline the specific conditions through which the engagement journey will be deemed completed. The acceptance criteria are most commonly found in the engagement's contract or statement of work. Being *done* is of critical importance because it is a legal matter. It defines the point at which the service provider can legally declare that the engagement is over. To do this, however, the service provider needs the customer to release them from the engagement environment, and it is unlikely that this will happen until the customer is happy that their expectations have been met. Until such a point, the two parties are legally bound to maintain the engagement environment regardless of the cost.

Maintaining a single vision of *done* is not easy when an engagement consists of so many different lines of communications. The number of two-way communications that must remain in alignment increase exponentially depending on the number of people (*n*) involved in the engagement at the rate of $(n \times (n - 1)) \div 2$. This means that for a small engagement of just 5 people, there will be 10 lines of communication that must remain aligned (i.e. $5 \times 4 \div 2$). An engagement of 10 people requires 45 lines of communication to be perfectly in sync, whereas an engagement team of 20 requires 190 lines of communication and (so on). Given this rate of expansion, you can easily see why maintaining just one single definition of *done* throughout an enterprise engagement can be such a challenge.

During an engagement, each team member generates their own database of emails, documents, and plans as a part of performing their role. Each new document creates a deeper and deeper level of detail that is required for the engagement, all of which help to identify how it is going to be successful. The detail and data created from the engagement can be so overwhelming that the original objectives can easily become obscured, or even worse, forgotten! Although a project manager is assigned the task of maintaining the engagement's vision of *done*, he or she will also be asked to deal with a lot of issues presented to them by the engagement teams. It is unfair to expect that it is *only* the project manager's responsibility to stay focused on *done*. For this reason, it is important that all team members adopt this principle. While a captain is in charge of the ship, it is the responsibility of the whole crew to keep it afloat by spotting dangerous obstacles, communicating them, and keeping the ship on a safe course.

You may be wondering why we use the term *"done"* instead of *"success"*? In most circumstances, *done* will indeed equate to *success* because that is the original objective of the professional services engagements. However, the original objective of all professional services engagements is also to supply services to customers for profit. When considering the end of an engagement we must remember that both the customer and the service provider entered into the agreement expecting for it to end in mutual success. The customer would get the business outcomes they wanted, and the service provider would make a profit.

However, sometimes the customer's vision of success can conflict with the service provider's view of success. This can happen if the customer's vision of success becomes too difficult or too costly for the service provider to deliver without further payments from the customer. At this stage, either the customer or the service provider may agree to alter the definition of *done* so that it no longer includes mutual success. In such a situation, it may be either or both parties who ultimately give up on a successful outcome. The result is that mutual success is no longer possible and someone (and potentially both teams) is now focused on being *done* rather than successful.

In an ideal world, all professional services engagements would end with mutual success. I wish that were true. However, the reality is that complex services engagements sometimes fail because of the nuanced challenges I present in this book. Although all service providers are resolute in their *desire* to deliver customer success, this principle can only be true in all circumstances if we use the term *done*. At the beginning of an engagement, the definition of *done* is success, but in some circumstances it must fall back to simply meaning finding a safe way out of the engagement environment. Many times, I have sacrificed profitability in order to retain a valued customer and exit the engagement environment safely. The problem, however, is that this cannot be the norm. A services firm that regularly achieves *done* without making money will not be in business for very long. Likewise, if the service provider focuses *only* on making money, they will soon get a reputation for not achieving customer success. This is the delicate tightrope that all service providers must walk.

THE CONTRACT: THE FIRST VERSION OF *DONE*

The first version of *done* is defined by the contract that initiates the engagement. Hence, if you have started working without a contract, then you have already gone against this principle. Whether you are delivering professional services as a profit center or a cost center, you *must* have some kind of an agreement with the customer that accurately identifies what *done* looks like. In its simplest form, this should include the following:

- A detailed description of the engagement (we call this the *Scope* of an engagement);

- The effort it is expected to take to achieve the scope;

- The price to be charged;

These three ways of describing *done* (scope, effort and time) are referred to as the triple constraints, and we will talk about them in detail later. For now, however, you must recognize them as being the basic building blocks for *done*. Think of them as being the solid outline of *done,* and everything else is just the detail inside the lines. The additional information the contract often provides with respect to defining *done* is as follows:

- How the two teams will objectively measure if the scope has been completed;

- Who is responsible for delivering the different components that constitute the scope of the contract;

- The process for changing the definition of *done*, if needed, during the engagement;

- Some definitions of *done* will add clarity by also stating what is not included within the scope of the engagement;

Combined with the triple constraints, these additional attributes create the first complete vision of *done* which, if achieved, will provide mutual success for both parties. You must read this document before starting to provide your services on any engagement. Researching your engagement's contract should become a part of your own personal best practice. It describes the outcome that you and the customer are trying to achieve within the engagement environment, and hence, is of critical importance in understanding how you can *expect* to deploy your technical skills.

Read the Contract

Ask for a condensed version of the contract (without all the legal jargon). If you are lucky, the bit that affects you is written into a part of the contract called the "Statement of Work" or "Work Order," which specifically defines the objective of the professional services you are to provide. To deliver successfully on your part of the engagement, it is essential to understand your organization's contractual commitments. As we will discuss in the next chapter, the most important elements of the contract are those that define the scope, effort, time and quality aspects of your engagement.

Understand the Customer's Desired Business Outcomes

As the contract progresses, make sure you understand exactly what the customer is trying to achieve. As the customer learns more from you, they are likely to change their definition of success, which may in turn change your own definition of what it means to be *done*. Although your customer's success is the ultimate goal, the contract price is based on your understanding of the customer's goal at the time the contract was signed, not the goal that may have formed as a result of subsequent conversations. If you are asked to begin work on something that is not covered by the contract, or you are asked to go back and rework something to achieve a different outcome, you need to alert your management team.

Don't let the customer intimidate you into doing work that is not stated in the contract. It may seem like just a small thing at the time, but if it snowballs and gets out of control, then you will be in the hot seat. All of these requests and variations to the original version of *done* need to be handled through a process called *Change Management*. While change management may not be your direct responsibility, you are a significant stakeholder in making sure that it is successfully executed and that all changes to *done* are correctly managed. An engagement that allows unmanaged changes to enter its work streams will always find it challenging to know exactly what *done* looks like.

Embrace the need for Change

Unlike the tightrope walker, the professional services equivalent of visualizing *done* is not as straightforward as making it across the wire safely. A professional services vision of *done* is complex and has many moving parts. While the contract is indeed the first version of *done*, you must understand that it is also a flawed vision. The contract is just an interpretation of the decision maker's desired business improvement and while it may be detailed and well constructed, it is rarely, if ever, a perfect description of what *done* will eventually look like.

As you progress through the engagement, you must take it upon yourself to confirm the contract's scope against the customer's desired business outcomes. Expect some inconsistencies and embrace the process of incorporating them into your work. While you are legally bound to deliver the solution defined in the contract, the customer is likely to need something slightly different to be truly successful. You must walk the delicate tightrope of adhering to the contract while also discovering the precise changes you need to make to it. We will discuss the techniques for managing contract change later in this chapter, but for now, just take not that change is to be expected.

Hold the Customer Accountable

Service providers often forget that the customer is also bound by the terms of the contract and has specific responsibilities within it. To that end, all members of the service provider's team should feel comfortable holding the customer accountable to the contract, but it must be done tactfully and courteously. Learn to respectfully remind the customer that you are all in this together. If the customer is acting in a way that places your mutual success at risk, then you should feel comfortable speaking up. It is ok to feel a little uncomfortable in this circumstance, but don't let the difficulty of any professional services conversation delay your action.

Too many times, I have had to clean up an engagement disaster that directly resulted from the service provider's failure to voice concerns about the customer's lack of accountability to the contract. You must be accountable to yourself and your firm to help prevent this situation. To do so, you must be aware of the commitments for which your customer is accountable. Typically, a customer commits to providing the following during an engagement:

- To provide you with access to the necessary customer employees or contractors to assist in making decisions or completing work products;

- To provide the appropriate number of people and resources to the engagement so that decisions can be made in a timely manner;

- To provide feedback on anything pertinent to achieving your outcomes in a timely manner;

- To provide a safe and professional work environment for your staff;

- To agree and sign off documents and specifications in a timely manner and to not hold them up unnecessarily;

- To pay for your services in accordance with the terms of the contract;

- To participate in good faith with a change management procedure;

This small list of commitments is enough for you to hold the customer accountable for the items you need to get the job *done*, and they are usually legally required to provide them to you. You must actively manage your customer and explain to them what you expect from them. If they do not meet with those expectations, then you must feel comfortable in reminding them of the importance of their role in the engagement's success.

Escalate Freely Within Your Team

You should also feel empowered to escalate to other members of your team whenever you see that either the customer or your firm is not adhering to the contract. Do not be afraid to escalate an issue to the appropriate person (usually your direct supervisor on the engagement). I have always recommended services executives encourage a policy that promotes the free escalation of any issue at any time during the engagement. Individuals within a service provider's team should know that if they see something that doesn't look right, they have the ability and responsibility to talk to their manager immediately. While some managers may feel as though time is wasted by these escalations, I believe that the policy of escalating freely saves enough time in avoiding future (and much larger) escalations to prove it worthwhile. By training your entire team on the principles of this book, you help to ensure that your team will reduce unfounded escalations, which results in the long-term benefit of saving time.

WHAT IF THERE IS NO CONTRACT?

There is a saying in the business of professional services that goes something like this: "You should never begin an engagement without a contract." For large professional services firms who earn hundreds of millions of dollars a year, this statement is 100% true. However, if you happen to work for a professional services firm that cannot afford to lose a customer's business, then this rule is only 99% true. These firms are frequently challenged to find a way to break this rule and win the customer's business. It is for this reason that the rule that you should never start without a contract is not identified as one of the core principles. While the rule should be upheld in *almost* all circumstances, there are indeed times when a professional services firm must take the very dangerous step of finding a way to break it. Some firms may do so for the following reasons:

- The customer wants to get started now because there is a deadline for the engagement to be completed;

- Negotiating the contract is taking longer than expected and the customer's deadline is driving an immediate start date;

- A competitor is willing to steal the business from the professional service firm by starting without a contract;

- If the professional services firm has consultants not being utilized then putting them to work early in the hope of being paid later, may be a risk the firm is willing to take;

Starting an engagement without a contract is likely not your decision. It is the decision of the managers and executives within your firm who will suffer the consequences should the endeavor fail. Never suggest to a customer that you can begin an engagement without a contract unless you have the express permission of a senior executive from your firm.

To help make the decision easier in this situation, some customers may suggest that you begin an engagement without a contract by signing something called a Letter of Intent (LOI) or a Memorandum of Understanding (MoU). However, it is important to note that these documents are not contracts and would not be recognized as a legally binding agreement in a court of law. In many cases, these kinds of agreements create more harm than good because they fail to cover important matters such as liability, dispute resolution, breach, and termination. Absent these details, courts are reluctant to enforce such documents regardless of them being signed.

There is a very good reason why some companies never break this rule. It is exceedingly dangerous, and it is rare that success eventuates. The issue however is not so much that success is rare, but that the cost of failure can be immense. Service providers have learned painfully, that engagements that start without a contract can become extremely costly, very quickly. Once work has begun, it is incredibly difficult to stop it. The respective teams have engaged and they are making progress towards the customer's desired outcomes. It can be very hard to extract the service provider's team without creating some element of damage to the customer relationship and potentially the service provider's own profit margins.

This is why many professional services firms agree that you should never start an engagement without a contract. However, the pressure to begin an engagement prior to signing the contract may become so significant that the rule may be justifiably broken. Although I strongly recommend against it, most professional services executive (including myself) have needed to break it at least once for the good of our firm. When doing so, there is a simple approach to breaking it successfully, and it begins with defining what *done* looks like.

In the case of starting an engagement without a contract, *done* is not the end point of your engagement, but the end point of the work you are going to undertake prior to the signing of a contract. By precisely defining the extent to which you are willing to commit to working on the customer's engagement, and by being crystal clear on what happens should the agreement remain unsigned once your efforts have been consumed, you have clearly defined what it means to be *done*. This provides you with a manageable way to move forward while mitigating some, but not all, of the associated risk of working without a contract.

Should it be necessary, these are the strict criteria I recommend for starting an engagement without a contract:

- Ask the customer for the specific date by which the contract will be signed. This date must come from the customer so that it represents *their* expectation of when they will sign the contract. You cannot set this date based on your expectations because the date by which the customer signs the contract is outside of your control. In a situation like this, you cannot commit to anything that you cannot control, and you must force the customer to feel accountable for providing the contract to you by the date they specified.

- Provide the customer with a set number of service hours prior to the signing of the contract. Typically, I wouldn't provide any more than 40-80 hours of services, and I would always keep the pre-contract effort to less than 10% of the total anticipated services hours for the entire engagement. You may also want to restrict the number and skill level of the resources available to the customer so that the engagement cannot progress too far before the contract is signed.

- In providing the small number of hours that were agreed upon, your team can attend meetings, take notes, and even do some work back at the office. Your team should not attend the customer's site, nor should they access any of the customer's electronic systems. Without a contract, there may be no legal protection for any damage you might cause to their systems. Similarly there is no insurance that would cover the costs of a workplace accident, if one were to occur.

- Other than publicly available materials, no other documentation, pre-existing or created specifically for the customer, should exchange hands. Documentation should never be provided to a customer until a contract has been signed. This includes timecard reports, status reports, and anything relevant to your internal best practices, your process, or information relating directly to the engagement. Without a contract, there is no agreement for the customer to pay for such valuable information. More importantly, there is also no law protecting what the customer can do with that information once they have it. That information is your company's important "know-how" (called *intellectual property*), and without a contract, it cannot be protected from plagiarism, inappropriate use, or even the possibility that your client could sell the information or misuse it.

- You should summarize all of this in an email and the customer should acknowledge the criteria you have set. While this is not a binding contract, it provides leverage that might withstand the scrutiny of an arbitration process sufficient that no customer would dare break it. This email should also include acknowledgement of the following.

  - If the contract is not signed by the committed date, then work will cease immediately;

  - If the agreed pre-contract hours are used then, work will cease immediately;

  - The hours you have worked prior to the signing of the contract will be rolled into the hours specified within it (hence, they will be paid for as a part of the contract once signed);

As you can see, the above criterion creates a mini-contract that makes it very clear about how and when the pre-contract work will be *done*. It creates a clear understanding that both parties are taking a risk by engaging without a contract, and that you will stop working on the engagement should the agreement not get signed on time. It also ensures that you are not providing the customer with anything of value given that they have not yet paid for anything. This approach limits your risk of the customer never paying for the cost of the hours you agreed to provide in advance of the signed contract.

While this is a well-planned approach, the hardest part about making this situation successful is actually executing it. Keeping control of an engagement environment once it is created is very difficult to do because it can easily take on a life of its own. If an experienced manager is not closely scrutinizing such a situation, it is incredibly easy for pre-contract work to expand from one person to five people within a few weeks. Therefore, due to the high level of risk involved in such an approach, it should only be executed by senior services managers because pausing a live engagement is incredibly difficult.

The customer will complain profusely, and you are going to feel very guilty for disrupting their progress. Your heart is going to tell you that another week or two isn't going to hurt, but the simple reality is that you *must* bring the engagement work to a halt if the contract is not signed as promised. Even if the customer escalates the issue and your team is told by your executives to re-engage in a few days, you should do so under the same criterion outlined above. The disruption you create will send a strong enough message that the customer will be unlikely to miss the deadline again. I have used this approach a number of times, and it has yet to fail me.

FIELD EXAMPLE: STARTING WITHOUT A CONTRACT

In fact, I was faced with this exact problem during the writing of this book. I had an account executive reach out to me and ask if we could start an engagement without a contract. We were a small startup in Silicon Valley, and we were trying to land a well-known customer in the face of competitors who were offering to provide their professional services for free! The account team and I were positive that if we held firm to the so-called golden rule, the deal would be lost. As this book was into its final drafts, I copied and pasted the criteria you have just read and sent them to the account executive. He walked the customer through them, and they agreed to get moving. We gave them one more week to get the contract signed, and we provided them with enough hours to have the engagement kick off.

When the time was up and the contract was not signed, the account executive called me. I was walking down Fifth Ave in New York at the time, and we had the difficult conversation about what to do. The account executive said the customer was pleading for another few days, and I declined. I explained that I wasn't trying to be difficult, but we had taken the risk and worked to a date set by the customer. It was time for the customer to be accountable for their promises. The account executive was very experienced, and while his heart was telling him to let the customer have another couple of days, he went back and delivered the difficult message. He called me the next day to say the customer was going to expedite the contract and have it signed and ready for us by the following business day.

This engagement ultimately ended in mutual success. The customer was very happy with our services, and it helped them achieve their desired outcomes. They employed us again later for more services because they respected the way we handled a very difficult situation. We were flexible within reason, but we also pushed them to *deliver on their commitments for the benefit of our mutual success. We walked the tightrope successfully, and we both reaped the rewards.*

PRESCRIBING *DONE*

As we have discussed throughout this book, you are the expert. As the expert, you have an opportunity to influence what *done* looks like. Most service providers ignore their ability to influence the outcome and instead persist in endlessly asking the customer what they want. The reality is that, for the customer to truly be successful, you must consider if what they *want* is what they really *need*. This isn't to say that customers don't know what they need, but it is a reminder that, as the expert, you have a responsibility to advise the customer if you feel that their *wants* and *needs* are misaligned.

In general, people will listen to an expert's recommendation. You have more sway than you may realize over the customer's decision-making process. If you can back your recommendation up with facts and experience, the customer will seriously consider it.

If you provide the customer with what they want and it does not lead to success, then how will that reflect upon you? If the customer feels as if you should have known better, then your ability to be trusted will evaporate. Saying "but that is what you asked for!" is not going to help you fix the situation. They are going to blame you for the lack of a successful outcome. Hence, you must understand your responsibility goes far beyond merely executing the customer's demands.

FIELD EXAMPLE: PRESCRIBING *DONE*

Here is another real life example from my experiences that demonstrates how prescription can assist you in avoiding future escalations. You must attempt to take this kind of approach when you know that the customer is heading in a troublesome direction and you are certain that there is a mutually beneficial alternative.

"I once worked for a software company that had a workflow approval engine that did not function as originally specified. The product included the ability to pass information around an organization for multiple approvals from different people. Approvals could be obtained in parallel (the information is sent to many people at once), or they could be obtained serially (the information is sent to one person who approves then forwards the information to another person for approval). Many customers naturally identified that using parallel approvals could mean faster overall approval times because approvals could be done simultaneously by all required approvers.

Despite the product's capacity to perform parallel approvals, it simply didn't work reliably. It would consistently break, which created a support nightmare. Once it broke, it was also incredibly complex and time-consuming to fix. We knew we had to fix the product but that was going to take a lot of time. So, as a company, we decided to stop implementing the parallel approval capability. We were very confident that this would result in a faster and higher quality implementation as well as a more stable and less troublesome support experience for our customers.

Shortly after telling our implementation team to only implement serial approvals, I received feedback that our customers were not listening to our advice because they were strongly in favor of parallel approvals. My team said they had asked the customer to reconsider their approach a number of times, but to no avail. The customer knew that this function was available in the product, and, in some instances, this was a factor in the customer's decision to select it. The issue was that we were asking if the customer wanted to move to serial approvals instead of prescribing that they should. Simply asking the customer was providing no real expertise. Our team was afraid to say, "If you choose parallel approvals, bad things will happen." While I can understand this fear, bad things were going to happen, so as the experts we had to make it our job to steer the customer away from this dangerous situation.

So as a team we trained ourselves to prescribe success. We began telling our customers that, although the product was capable of serial and parallel workflows, our experience (based on more than one hundred implementations) was that parallel workflows were not worth implementing. They were hard to design and deploy, and once in use, they would frequently break, resulting in costly repairs. We told the customer that we strongly recommended using serial approvals, and that our implementation teams had been instructed not to implement parallel approvals without obtaining permission from the Senior Vice President of Customer Success (that was me). By doing this, we created a very strong recommendation that the customer could not ignore. We were never going to simply tell a customer that we wouldn't implement parallel workflows, but we had to demonstrate that we took their success sufficiently serious that we required executive approval to do so. By doing this, we ensured that if the customer wanted to go against our *recommendation, they would receive a thorough description of the potential consequences.*

The difference was amazing. As experts, the customers trusted our experience in implementing the process, and they almost always went with our prescription of what the final solution should look like. A few customers pushed back on the serial approvals recommendation by telling us that they were the exception to the rule, and that they needed parallel approvals. When this happened, we told them that we appreciated how they felt, and then offered to let them talk to other customers who had initially thought the same way only to choose serial approvals and find them more effective. This opened up the possibility that the customer's situation was not as unique as they believed. In all remaining instances, the customer declined and simply agreed to employ the serial approval.

We probably faced this scenario thirty times or so. Each customer expected parallel workflows, and we only needed to go beyond the prescriptive recommendation a handful of times. Customers never insisted we implement parallel workflows for them—not once! Once implemented, our customers were delighted with the serial approvals process as it worked consistently. We never had a single complaint that serial approvals were not adequate. This real life example illustrates that prescribing success to your customer will drastically improve your chances of achieving it, even when the customer may prefer an alternative approach."

I have no doubt that this single shift in how we assisted the customer in defining the finished solution saved us hundreds of support tickets and thousands of hours trying to resolve customer issues related to parallel workflows-- not to mention that the customer received a more reliable solution because it worked correctly every time. If your customers trust you, they will want you to lead them to their desired outcomes. If they do not, they will argue with your recommendations. Prescription can both earn your customer's trust and achieve a more successful outcome. If being prescriptive could help you achieve customer success more efficiently, why wouldn't you do it?

While there is no Hippocratic Oath for professional services consultants, we must consider the same issues doctors face when prescribing medicines for their patients. Our job as a consultant is to do right by the customer, not by ourselves. The power of prescription should never be misused. If a misuse is discovered, it will surely result in the complete loss of any customer's trust in you, and it would signal the last time your firm ever works with that customer again. On the other hand, when the power of prescription is used correctly, it will save your engagement and provide your customer with the successful outcome they wanted, but in a different way than expected.

CHANGING *DONE*: BASELINES AND CHANGE MANAGEMENT

To further complicate the clarity of what it means to be *done*, the customer's expectations of success may shift several times during an engagement. If these shifts are not uniformly communicated and understood by both the customer and the service provider, then misalignment is imminent and a successful outcome is unlikely. Managing any change to the definition of *done* is critical for the engagement to know exactly where it is heading. The general term for this process is called *Change Management*.

As you can imagine, each change to *done* also creates a new and differing *version* of it. Just like if you edit "Draft 1" of a document it now becomes "Draft 2." You can think of it as if you are altering *Done 1.0* so that it now becomes *Done 1.1*. The process of managing these versions is called *Version Control*. Almost anything can be versioned: the initial contract, a subsequent project plan, a design document, a spreadsheet, or a piece of software. These items that are version controlled are called *engagement assets*, as they are valuable items created by the engagement process. Each new version of an asset receives a unique identifier known as a version number, so there is an easy way to tell the versions apart. In a services engagement, it is likely that many items will be versioned. This includes those documents that make up the complete description of what *done* will look like.

As the engagement assets are changed and versioned, it can become very difficult to understand which version defines *done*. Sometimes there can be more than ten versions of an asset created, each of which go through a process of being created, finalized, reviewed, and ultimately either being accepted as approved or rejected. While an asset version may have several statuses throughout its lifecycle, there is only one status that is important to the definition of *done* and that is the status of being *approved*. Until an engagement asset receives the *approved* status, it has not officially changed the definition of *done*. With all of these versions of engagement assets floating around, it can be very difficult to keep track of them all. To avoid confusion with respect to which versions are those that have been agreed as defining *done* for an engagement, the industry uses an approach called *baselining*.

A baseline is simply the assignment of one specific version of an asset (or multiple assets) as *the* current version that represents *done*. While many other versions of an asset may exist, nobody should be considering any other version as relevant to the definition of *done* unless it is declared as the current baseline. To illustrate how this might work, lets take the example of building a house. In this example there are several documents that combine to define *done*.

Engagement Assets	Purpose
Master Plan	Defines the overall vision of both the house and gardens as a single vision.
Floor Plan (Blueprint)	Defines the structural components of the house.
Electrical Plan	Defines the wiring components of the house and the garden area.
Landscaping Plan	Defines the detail of each garden bed.

At the start of the construction project, these documents are provided to the customer who agrees that they define *done*, so he or she signs the contract. At this point, the contract consists of four plans, all of which have only one version and are all considered a part of the project's current baseline. During the construction, however, the master builder hits several issues that require him to re-plan certain elements of both the house and the gardens. Added to this, the customer asks for some changes to elements such as electricity outlets, some different plants for a garden bed, etc. After a few months, the version control for each document (we can think of them as engagement asset) may look something like this.

Engagement Assets	Version Control History (Status)
Master Plan	Version 1.0 Original plan (Approved) Version 1.1 Amendments for foundation adjustments (Draft) Version 1.2 Amendments for alarm system changes (Draft) ***Version 1.3 Amendment for adding the garden pergola and foundation adjustment (Approved – Current Baseline)***
Floor Plan / Blueprint	Version 1.0 Original plan (Approved) Version 1.1 Amendments for foundation adjustments (Approved) ***Version 1.2 Amendment for different door placements (Approved – Current Baseline)***
Electrical Plan	***Version 1.0 Original plan (Approved – Current Baseline)*** Version 1.1 Amendments for alarm system changes (Draft)
Landscaping Plan	Version 1.0 Original plan (Approved) ***Version 1.1 Amendments for foundation adjustments (Approved – Current Baseline)***

For each document above, the **bold italicized** version represents the current baseline, which also corresponds to the most recently *approved asset by the customer*. In this example, *done* is defined by version 1.3 of the Master Plan, version 1.2 of the Floor Plan, version 1.0 of the Electrical Plan, and version 1.1 of the Landscaping Plan. You will notice that these are the most recently *approved* versions of each of the plans. Previously approved versions of the plans are no longer a part of the baseline because new baselines have been agreed upon with the customer. Once a new version is approved, it becomes the current baseline version until a later version is approved.

Notice that those documents in *draft* status are not included in the baseline because the customer has not approved them, and they should not be used as a guide for any work being done on the construction site. Changes have to go through a draft stage because somebody has to evaluate the impact of the requested changes and provide them to the customer for review. The change in plans is likely to come with a change in price and time required for the plan to be delivered. The customer must consider all of these before agreeing to them and approving them. It is quite common for drafts to never be approved.

The process of maintaining a single version of *done* by baselining multiple engagement assets is referred to as *configuration management*. As an example, if each asset above was changed and approved independently of the others, then *done* has been changed four times since the initial agreements and, hence, we would have had four different configurations of *done*.

Although the concept of baselining is straightforward, it is incredibly valuable for maintaining a clear definition of *done*. With so many documents and other assets being created on a large engagement, you can see how a team might begin to lose track of which versions should be driving their activities. You would be surprised how often this happens. The hectic nature of customer engagements can make this kind of rigor seem unimportant and team members stop adhering to it. Some people like to think that version control and change management are owned solely by the project manager and will expect him or her to take care of it.

The reality, however, is that every team member must understand how this ongoing management of assets affects their ability to focus on *done*. If you are the author of a key engagement asset, then you are the one responsible for the management and communication of the current baseline version. Even if you are not the author of a document, you must still ensure that you only ever work from current baselines and that you also identify situations where non-baselined versions of engagement assets are being used incorrectly. An engagement has the greatest chance of success when the entire team holds themselves accountable for maintaining the collective vision of *done*.

The use of version control, baselines, and change management creates a manageable way for a service provider and customer to change their version of *done* while not unnecessarily distracting the team members. The use of version control, baselines, and change management are critical to always knowing what *done* looks like. Make sure that you are aware of how they are being used on your engagement. Without them, you are putting your customer and yourself at risk.

PREPARING TO BE *DONE* – CUSTOMER ACCEPTANCE TESTING

Always knowing what *done* looks like is only effective if you are able to finally achieve the result of being *done*. To achieve this result you must remember that most professional services contracts provide the customer with the right to *accept* or *reject* the quality and accuracy of your work. This is where it can be difficult for the customer and the service provider to agree upon the precise definition of *done*. Given the commitment your customer stakeholders have made about the outcomes your engagement will achieve, they are likely to view acceptance through the lens of those commitments rather than through the lens of the current baselined version of *done*. This is both common and understandable. It is easier for a customer to imagine the benefits of your engagement than to review each specific contract term and identify if those benefits are accurately detailed by the scope and specifications they had previously agreed with you.

Think of it this way. Imagine you asked a contractor to build you a chair. You specify as much as you can about that chair including the style of it, the material with which it is to be made, and its dimensions. Eventually the contractor is done and he shows it to you. While your contractor may have met precisely with all of the requirements you gave him, there are still several other elements that you may be unhappy with. For instance, it may be uncomfortable to sit in. The cushion material may not feel comfortable. You may not like the way that your contractor rounded the arms or the back of the chair. Even on simple items there are nuances and criteria that are often difficult to describe or easily overlooked at the time the requirements were agreed. On large and complex services engagements, there could be hundreds of items that were not specific in the original contract that your customer may decide are important enough to declare your work unacceptable.

You must anticipate this reaction throughout your engagement. When your customer sees your work for the first time, they are going to compare it to their expectations of what they believed they asked for. Even though your work may have been completed exactly as requested you and your customer may not agree on the precise definition of *done*. The variance between your customer's expectation of your engagement's outcomes and the work you finally show them will determine the degree to which this difference in opinion becomes an issue. Hence, it is wise to try and identify these gaps as early as possible to prevent them from becoming so wide at the conclusion of your engagement that they hold up acceptance. It is likely that by the letter of your contract, you are only *done* once your customer has accepted your work. To achieve this I recommend the following techniques:

Frequent Check-Ins

Highly iterative engagement models such as Agile or Rapid Prototyping are popular because they allow the service provider to demonstrate the preliminary results of their work effort to their customer on a regular and consistent basis. This proactive approach helps ensure that any misalignments with the customer's expectations are spotted early. However, in this situation the fact that the work is incomplete means that the customer can only provide feedback on whether or not it is *heading in the right direction.* This is not the same as providing actual acceptance because all customers want to see the completed piece of work before they agree that it has been *done.* But it has proven to be so valuable for preventing large gaps at acceptance, it has become a very popular approach during many types of engagements in recent times.

In the example above, the customer could check in with the contractor and see how the construction of the chair is progressing. During such a check-in the customer may point out that the way the contractor has constructed the first of the chair's arms does not meet with their satisfaction, and the contract then has the ability to adjust his approach without too much additional cost.

As we have already discussed in this chapter, during these check-ins, you must remember to stay focused on the current baseline that defines *done.* You must identify any differences between the customer's expectation and the definition of *done* as per the contract or specifications you are using and determine how to handle that difference. With such frequent check-ins, it is possible to inch slowly away from the original definition of *done* without noticing it until the point that the misalignment becomes so noticeable that it causes an escalation.

Customer Written Acceptance Tests

Customers must also generate their own acceptance tests and share them with the service provider. I cannot tell you how often I have come across customers that expect the service provider to write these tests when in fact they are clearly the customer's responsibility. While having the service provider write the tests would be easier for the customer, a service provider will never anticipate the definition of *done* sufficiently. In comparison to the customer's wealth of knowledge about his or her own business, the service provider usually has less. Hence, tests written by the service provider are insufficient because they only test for the outcomes the customer has already specified. Instead, a test written by the customer will be more carefully written, and the detail it provides will likely lead to a much better definition of what is expected of being *done.*

Considering our example above, the customer may identify that lumbar support is a critical acceptance criteria. The customer knows that they have a propensity to suffer from back pain and hence a chair that provides poor support will not be comfortable. It is these kinds of nuances that get missed at the time of the original specification because they are not obvious and often not even considered by the service provider.

The use of this technique frequently results in the discovery of small variations, and the customer frequently identifies situations that they and the service provider have not previously considered. While these discoveries lead to difficult conversations about scope and how to incorporate them into the baseline, it is better to discover them during the process than to discover them after the fact because it is cheaper for the service provider to adjust to meet with them.

When a customer does agree to write their own tests, they must share them with you, as well as the expected results. I encounter a surprising number of customers who will write their own tests but neglect to share either the tests or the results they expect with the service provider. Their rationale is that sharing them will make it too easy for the service provider to pass them. The reality is that these test cases and expected results serve the best example the service provider has of what *done* looks like. To manipulate the outcomes so they met only with the results provided and still not meet with the customer's expectations would not only be an extraordinary amount of additional, but could also be grounds for the customer to claim fraudulent behavior by the service provider.

When this happens, you must address the customer's fear. There is nothing to be gained by the service provider in delivering their outcomes so that they *only* pass the tests provided by the customer. Given the late stage at which these tests are usually provided, this would be a very hard thing for the service provider to do. Sharing the tests with the service provider beforehand ensures that the complete battery of tests accurately reflects the definition of *done* from which the service provider has been working. It is far better to do this in advance than to leave this discovery until the very late stages of the engagement.

Partial or Conditional Acceptance

Once a piece of work is being tested, there are likely to be many conversations about small issues that are preventing its acceptance. Service providers can often forget to ask for partial or conditional acceptance of their work because they are more focused on the bigger picture of *done*. When the service provider can document that some work has been accepted and other parts are not, this is known as a *Partial Acceptance*. This ability to partially accept the work means that the service provider is constantly making progress towards acceptance of the whole. Although it took me many years to realize it, our industry should embrace the premise that a customer's "partial" acceptance of work is a step in the right direction.

An even better approach operates on the theory that work may be conditionally accepted. Many customers will continue to operate on the premise that if any portion of the work is not accepted, then all of the work is unacceptable. In this situation, you can strongly recommend that the customer accept the whole work product under the condition that you provide a reasonable number of hours effort to complete the outstanding items. We will discuss why a customer might be willing to agree to this in the next section.

The aim of partial and conditional acceptances is to have the customer agree that a subset of the work is completed. In obtaining these acceptances, the service provider continues to formally complete parts of the engagement while agreeing that the customer can now only object to those items that have not been accepted.

LEVERAGING ACCEPTANCE

You may be wondering why a customer would agree to accept something partially or conditionally? A customer's instinctive reaction is to hold the entire engagement up as being unacceptable until every aspect of the engagement has met with their expectations. This is a fairly natural reaction as the customer is trying to use their acceptance of the whole engagement as leverage to make the service provider continue to do work for them. The customer will argue that once *everything* is completed to their satisfaction, they will accept the whole engagement as being *done*. While this seems like a fair reaction, many service providers and consultants mishandle the situation by forgetting the leverage they also possess.

The leverage that the service provider possesses is the ownership of the final work product itself. In the example I used above, that final work product would be the chair. Hence, the service provider should ensure that the customer does not take possession of the chair until such a point that they agree that all of its specifications are correct and are acceptable to the customer. The customer wants the chair and is likely to be excited to take possession of it. Hence, the motivation for the customer to object to any of the chairs specifics will be considered carefully. This approach forces the customer to put any objections about the work product in perspective and not unfairly hold up the acceptance of the whole because of an insignificant issue they may have with a small part of it. Additionally, in enterprise professional services engagements, the customer's stakeholders have promised considerable improvements to their executives. The longer the engagement continues without providing the promised improvements, the more anxious these executives will become, and the more likely the customer's stakeholders will be to accept minor imperfections in your work because it is insignificant in comparison with agreeing to be *done*.

In order to get your customer's attention and cooperation at the time of acceptance, you must leverage this pressure. By retaining possession of your work products and insisting that the customer consider the significance of their objections to acceptance, you and your firm ensure that acceptance is only reasonably withheld if you have materially failed to deliver upon your commitments. Your goal is to synchronize the acceptance of your work with the customer's ability to use the work product you created, and hence, simultaneously relinquishing you from your contractual obligations.

You should always ensure that you maintain possession of your final work product until the customer accepts it. Once a customer take possession of a work item without accepting it, the service provider's ability to leverage acceptance is completely lost.

FIELD EXAMPLE: NOBODY KNEW WHAT *DONE* LOOKED LIKE!

As we have discussed, there is a seemingly infinite stream of communication taking place on a complex engagement, including a myriad of emails, documents, issues, and requests (often in multiple versions). I have learned the hard way that teams can easily become so engrossed in these details that they lose sight of the big picture. Once this happens, the definition of *done* can become different for almost everybody on the engagement. It only takes one person to begin creating his or her own version of *done* for the engagement to begin to veer off course.

One morning, I arrived at work to see one of our project teams frantically working to fix errors in a piece of software that was due to be provided to an important customer that day. The customer was testing our software and sending back a raft of issues so the situation was escalating quickly. The most significant of these issues was that, after several failed attempts to provide the software to the customer, it was still not passing their tests. It was one of those crazy mornings where the world was on fire but nobody could find a hose. I joined the team and quickly reviewed the list of issues with the project manager. Today was the deadline for delivery, and if we didn't give them a working version of our software, it was surely going to escalate to their executives.

After our first review of the outstanding issues, I stepped back to look at the big picture. I posed the question as to why our software wasn't working? Our project manager responded that he didn't know because he hadn't seen the actual tests that the customer was using to determine if our software was acceptable. Having contemplated the issue in a larger context, I posed a simple question: if we have not seen the criteria by which the customer is trying to accept the software, then how could we have ever built it to meet with their expectation? After a quick check of our design specification with a handful of the customer's tests, we identified that they were both clearly misaligned.

The customer was very upset that the software was failing their tests because they were under pressure to get it in front of their business users-- to whom they had been promising it for months! If they missed their committed date to launch the new product to their users, then the next available date to try it again was not for another 4 weeks. They were already late and over budget, so they were facing immense pressure from their own internal stakeholders to deliver something now.

I decided that it was time to make the difficult phone call to the customer's executive sponsor. If the customer was testing the software against a set of tests that we had never seen, then it was almost impossible for those tests and our original specifications to be defining the same version of done. We already had several proof points that the failing tests were never mentioned in our agreed design specification, so we could continue to chase our tails or do the right thing and stop the madness. She was a very professional and pragmatic woman who happened to be travelling in Asia at the time. She was also in the middle of fielding very difficult questions from her executives in the U.S. who wanted to know if and when the new solution was going to be launched to their employees.

"I think it is best to agree that we have missed this deadline," I explained. As both teams were still frantically working to meet it, this was a difficult thing to propose. Given the fact that we were being held accountable to successfully pass tests that we had never seen during the implementation process, a successful outcome by the end of the day was not possible. This was analogous to being asked to build a toaster and then being measured by a test to see if it could produce good coffee! I explained that the miscommunication between our respective teams had resulted in none of us knowing what done was meant to look like. This resonated with her and, at that point, we mutually agreed to stop the engagement and regroup when she returned to the United States.

After this event, there were weeks of critical meetings. The customer had spent one million dollars to get this solution up and running, and about a quarter of that was paying our team to build it. But our failure to mutually manage what done looked like had cost the customer far more than just money. Our executive sponsor had to go back to the Chief Financial Officer (CFO) and explain why her investment in our products and services had resulted in zero business improvement. At the same time, the customer *had to make a decision: spend at least another quarter of a million dollars on attempting to rebuild the solution with us again, or simply abandon the endeavor, which meant they would lose the one million dollars they had already invested. Having to explain this situation to the customer's CFO would have been uncomfortable, and I was quite glad I didn't have to be there.*

Thankfully, over time we were able to rebuild the relationship with our customer and provide them with a quality solution. There were lots of uncomfortable conversations, but, fortunately, the customer proved very pragmatic. Despite the solution's complexity, they agreed that this situation should never have happened. They also understood that both teams could have worked better to ensure that the focus on done was not lost. They were willing to work with us to get the solution delivery back on track, despite the additional investment it required. While we did eventually correct the situation, it is hard to say if we ever really regained the customer's trust.

This example highlights the damage that can be caused when a team loses site of *done*. It is easy for an individual consultant to say "it's not my job" and let important issues go unchecked. If just one consultant on either team had thought to check whether the two teams were working on the same version of *done*, then this situation may have been avoided. It is likewise easy to say "I'd never let it get that far," but the reality is that, under the immense pressure of tight deadlines, it is incredibly hard to be that one person who pushes against the tsunami and says "Stop!" However, for the good of your career and your firm, you must learn to become comfortable being that person. It is imperative to the success of every engagement you work on. If you're unclear *at any point* on what it means to be *done*, you must speak up!

CHAPTER SUMMARY

Don't forget that you're on the tightrope for the duration of the engagement. Don't permit yourself to become distracted by irrelevant details that will prevent you from successfully reaching the other side. Permitting distractions from superfluous details in the middle of the engagement can cost you your balance and result in a damaging fall. If you and your customer share the same understanding of *done*, then your chances of reaching the other side of your tightrope are vastly improved. By the same token, your customers are also on a tightrope, and your destinies are mutually intertwined. If one of you falls, there are consequences for both of you. Obviously, you need to maintain your own balance, but at the same time, your expert status makes you responsible to help your customers keep theirs. Although you don't fully control your customer's destiny, you must employ your expertise to their advantage, and always make your best effort to help them successfully cross their own tightrope.

MANAGE EXPECTATIONS

"The expectations of life depend upon diligence; the mechanic that would perfect his work must first sharpen his tools."

– Confucius

GREAT EXPECTATIONS

Together, the principles of *Adapt to Your Environment* and *Always Know What Done Looks Like* provide you the foundational skills necessary to step out onto the professional services tightrope and keep your balance. Now we will examine more of the skills necessary to maintain your balance as you walk across it. Despite the inherent dangers, tightrope walkers will continually push themselves to improve the quality of their act. If the performance is repetitive, the audience will become bored. By the same token, if the performer exceeds his physical limits, then the risk of injury skyrockets. Hence, he must continue to improve the allure of his death-defying act while simultaneously maintaining his safety.

Likewise, the professional services consultant must convince the customer that the engagement's outcome is worth funding, while at the same time, insuring that the outcome is achievable. If you begin with low expectations, the customer will be underwhelmed and unlikely to see the return on investment. If you inflate the engagement's expected outcomes, then it is unlikely you'll be able to deliver them, and you'll have an even bigger disaster on your hands. This disaster will undermine your chance of any future business with that customer, and you will not reach the trusted advisor status.

The customer expects that you will make them successful in return for the fee you are collecting. Hence, balancing their expectations of success with your abilities to deliver it is one of critical importance.

An *expectation* is a belief that somebody will achieve *something* in the future. While this definition can seem open and subjective, to the professional services provider that *something* is *customer success*. To achieve customer success, you will need to deliver many smaller "somethings" to your customer's exact expectation. This chapter is about making sure you know how to manage those expectations. This principle will help you understand what a customer expects of you *before* you begin, how your actions will shape a customer's expectations, and finally, how to set your customer's expectations accurately.

Like most of the principles in this book, this concept focuses on the nuance of an obvious premise. Everyone knows that we should set realistic expectations, and yet we frequently fail to do so. The simple fact is that setting expectations accurately within a high-pressure engagement environment requires vigilance and practice. This chapter will help you understand how expectations are set, which in turn will help you identify when you must take action to manage and adjust them appropriately. Doing this correctly will help you complete your engagement successfully.

MANAGING INHERENT EXPECTATIONS

Most engagements begin with an important meeting we call the *Engagement Kick Off*. This meeting usually outlines the basic expectations that each party has of the engagement. At this kick-off, the customer's team already has expectations of your team and the voyage upon which you are about to take them. These are called *inherent* expectations, and though you have done nothing to deserve them, the customer has these preconceptions from the minute you walk in the door. They are not based on any first-hand experience with you, but they are primarily (although not solely) formed by their experiences during your sales process.

Your sales team had to win this customer's business. There is no doubt they have pitched you as a service provider of outstanding quality. They may have also had to provide a winning *yestimate* to secure the customer's business. Your customer is already expecting a high level of quality from you regardless of the final price that may have been negotiated. In addition, your customer will have prior experience with professional services consultants, both positive and negative. All of these experiences will influence their inherent expectations of you. Due to the influence of experience on these inherent expectations, it is likely that each of the customer's team members will have a slightly different expectation of what you are about to do. This is why the alignment of expectations at the engagement kick off is so important.

The engagement kick off is your first opportunity to understand and react to these expectations. As a part of this exercise, you must identify the customer's inherent expectations and decide whether you can deliver to them, or whether their expectations will need to be adjusted. Success is only possible if you meet your customer's expectations, so this is an important decision. If you fail to identify and manage the inherent expectations immediately, the engagement will start off on the wrong foot, and you may never recover.

To ensure success at the engagement kick off, you must spend time preparing for it. First, you must understand the situation you are walking into and begin applying the first principle of *Adapt to Your Environment.* To achieve this, it's important to meet with your sales team before the kick off and get a complete understanding of the events that have transpired prior to your involvement as well as any other observations they may have about the customer's environment. This meeting is typically known as the *Sales-to-Services Handover,* and it should be a well-structured walkthrough of how your sales team landed the deal. It should inform your entire engagement team of how the sales process was handled, the commitments that were made, and what they believe the customer is expecting of you once the engagement begins. This provides you with the background information you are going to need in order to align those inherent expectations.

The sales-to-services handover meeting should detail the customer's expected business outcomes, the key stakeholder's backgrounds, their responsibilities and the agreed budget of the engagement. Any unusual contract terms should also be discussed so that your team is fully prepared to alter its usual approach within the engagement environment if necessary. A well-run handover meeting provides the services team the best possible understanding of the environment they are walking into as well as the best possible idea of what *done* looks like before meeting with the customer.

In some complex engagements, it may even be worth holding a *Kick Off Preparation Meeting* with your customer after the sales-to-services handover. Too often, customers arrive at the kick off expecting the services team to perform a quick magic show and immediately bring clarity to a complex problem. If you believe you are at risk of this, it is wise to have a kick off preparation meeting with the customer to set clear expectations about the objectives of the kick off meeting. This will allow you to communicate your expectations of the meeting and get a sense of whether or not they align with the customers. A worthwhile kick off is likely to require that the customer's team bring specific information about their business to the meeting. This information helps the service provider's team get oriented in the newly formed engagement environment. If you do not share this expectation with the customer, they will not bring this information to the meeting, and you will immediately begin to set the engagement back. A customer kick off preparation meeting is always valuable, but for complex engagements it is a must.

Once you've adequately prepared the customer for the kick-off, you're ready to get it started. The engagement kick off provides the first opportunity for the respective team members to meet each other. These teams are going to have a great deal of interaction in the coming weeks or maybe months, so this meeting is always more effective when done face-to-face. Although the engagement kick off can be held over the phone or teleconference, your experience over time will highlight that this is always a less effective method. However it is done, you must make sure that adequate time is provided for each team member to introduce themselves so that the team can become familiar with each other and, hence, enhance how they communicate from this point forward.

Although the engagement kick off agenda may vary from company to company, it should at a minimum include the following:

- Introduce team members and their roles and responsibilities;

- Introduce the engagement's methodology and draft plan;

- Summarize the contract's scope (the first version of what *done* will look like);

- Summarize how the engagement team will know that the engagement is *done* (e.g. define acceptance criteria, describe the outcomes that will have been achieved, etc.);

- Summarize the baseline, issue, risk and change management processes;

- Summarize the project planning and communications processes;

- Identify any urgent issues or risks;

- Identify any immediate next steps to get the engagement off and running;

As you can see, a great engagement kick off does not occur by accident. Success requires considerable planning and preparation. A poorly planned or rushed kick off will set you back weeks, and you'll be stuck trying to repair the damage and regain the customer's trust. There is no need to falter at this step, and you can easily avoid doing so simply by properly planning and preparing. Finishing an engagement successfully is hard enough without unnecessarily hampering yourself at the start.

BALANCING EXPECTATIONS: THE TRIPLE CONSTRAINTS

Without a doubt, the customer's most critical expectations at the beginning of an engagement are those written into your contract. Contracts typically do this by detailing the *scope* of your engagement, the necessary *effort* required for you and your customer to achieve it, and the expected *time* (engagement duration) for that effort to be exerted. These elements are known as the *Triple Constraints,* and they are bound together by a relationship known as *The Law of the Triple Constraints.*

This law states that, in an engagement, these three elements combine together to create the overall quality of the service being provided. You can consider that the measure in which these three ingredients are delivered within an engagement will determine the overall quality of the service provided. This inter-dependence means that, if any one ingredient shifts during the course of an engagement, the others must also shift proportionally to compensate and ensure that the level of quality is retained. If the other ingredients do not shift then the resultant quality is going to vary.

For example, when a customer wants to expand the scope of an engagement, they may not realize that this will also require more effort than originally estimated. To retain the original level of quality, the other constraints must also change. More scope means more effort and, most likely, more time. Agreeing to add scope without adjusting effort and time will only deteriorate the quality of the engagement's outcomes. Customers often seek to change one of these elements during an engagement without changing the others in the hope that the engagements price does not increase. This is a reasonable desire given that an increase may mean having to go back to the CFO to beg for more money, and nobody looks forward to that. Hence, it is imperative that you understand this law so you can help align your customer's expectations.

The Law of the Triple Constraints is represented in the following way.

This triangle illustrates that Quality is the outcome of applying Scope, Effort and Time (The Triple Constraints) together in an engagement. Once the quantity of each of these elements is established in the contract, a shift in any one of them will require a shift in the others in order to maintain the same level of quality throughout the engagement.

It is critical to understand these dynamics so that you can clearly explain them to a customer. To give you some further examples, this law will clarify why you're unable to reduce the engagement's cost without reducing the engagement's scope unless the customer is willing to accept an outcome of lesser quality. The triple constraints will help you clarify why this must happen. To lessen the cost of the engagement, we would have to reduce effort and bill fewer hours. The law states that this, in turn, would reduce the quality of the engagement because the scope did not shift proportionally to the effort.

While a service provider could decide to reduce the hourly billing rate in order to reduce the customer's price, the purpose of the triple constraints is not to justify commercial pricing decisions, but to reflect the real world dependencies that these elements have on each other. Commercial pricing is entirely up to the service provider and is based on desired financial outcomes. The triple constraints apply only to the physical relationship between scope, effort and time.

Once the constraints are established, there is no free lunch. If one expectation shifts, the others must also shift. Understanding this law will give you the ability to explain it to your customers, which will help focus the conversation on working within the law rather than trying to break it. To ensure that you understand the elements of this law completely, I have included a detailed definition of each below.

Scope

Scope means the depth and breadth of the work that needs to be completed. It may be described in terms of activities that need to be completed, or a specific set of deliverables that will be provided to the customer by the engagement's completion. Knowing the scope of an engagement is so important that it has its own principle in the form of *Always Know What Done Looks Like*. Frequently, the scope section of an engagement's contract lacks detail, as the customer is still unaware of what they want exactly. For this reason, you should be prepared to identify any misaligned expectations. It is better to address these issues as soon as possible because without aligning these expectations, you and your customer have a different understanding of what *Done* looks like.

Effort

The effort refers to the total use of resources (human or otherwise) required to complete the scope of the engagement. Effort can take the form of service hours to be consumed by the engagement, or other resources, such as hardware, software, or building materials. People often use the term cost to describe this element rather than effort, but I prefer to measure resources by their raw quantities (e.g. hours, number of servers, etc.) rather than derived quantities such as dollars. Cost and price are both derived from effort by assigning a dollar value to each unit and then multiplying it by the number of units being used.

For example, 20 hours of consulting effort may be priced at $4000 ($200 an hour). In this example, the price may be discounted to $3000 by changing the hourly rate to $150 an hour for purposes of winning the contract. Hence, the price has been reduced but the effort remains the same. To further the example, the cost of the engagement is derived from the unit cost of the resource being used. We can reduce the cost of the engagement by using offshore resources at a cost of $45 an hour instead of the local rate of $90 an hour. While this reduces the cost of the engagement, the effort remains the same. Given the commercial flexibility of terms like cost and price, I believe that the law applies directly to effort and indirectly to all other derivatives of it.

Time (Duration)
Time refers to the number of calendar days required to complete the *scope* by deploying the requisite *effort*. When calculating this variable, we assume that the engagement plan has been optimized, which means that there is no unnecessary slack or downtime. In other words, there is no possibility of rearranging the order of the tasks or scheduling of the resources that would make the duration of the engagement shorter.

Quality
Quality is not a constraint. Instead, it is the resultant product of the three constraints combined. Specifically, quality results from the effort you applied to the scope of the project over the specified period of time. Some quality is measurable

and some quality is subjective. The degree to which you can identify and measure quality will vary based on the type of engagement you are delivering. Regardless of the level of quality, the Law of the Triple Constraints holds that you cannot maintain the expected level of quality of a professional services outcome if one of the elements is changed, unless you change the other variables proportionally.

The Exception?

Over the years, I've thought long and hard about the Law of Triple Constraints, and I've discovered one flaw that you should be aware of: the law does not always adjust for the impact of technical innovation or the reuse of existing intellectual property. In my estimation, these are the only ways to adjust one of the variables without impacting the others. For example, a new computer program may make it possible to achieve an outcome in 20 hours that previously required 100 hours of effort. This would reduce the effort without undermining the engagement's quality (it may in fact improve it).

In the same way, a prepackaged service may fast track a complex process and in turn increase the scope that can be completed within a given timeframe by reusing existing know-how. In other words, a template driven service offering may achieve the same level of quality for a larger amount of scope in the same or shorter period of time.

This continual improvement in what we can accomplish in the same period of time is similar to the process of commoditization. Commoditization occurs in almost all areas of product manufacturing where valuable and hard to make products become cheaper and easier to make over time. While less prevalent in the services industry, this natural evolution of improvement occurs because of the constant need to improve the value we offer to our customers. Although the services we offer are less susceptible to technological change and improvements in intellectual property, it still happens.

This is important to understand because your competitors are constantly trying to find ways to provide your customers with a better service than you, so be aware! If they can maintain or improve the quality of an engagement by applying better technology or reusing their own intellectual property, they may soon be offering a more compelling service than you can provide. For this reason, it is important to constantly assess new ways to deliver your services. This helps you be the first to get the competitive advantage if there is one to be had.

There is plenty of external literature on the Triple Constraints, and you should certainly consider further reading on the subject. In some cases, it is referred to as the *Project Management Triangle*, or even the *Iron Triangle*. If you are interested in developing your understanding of this subject, you might begin by studying the field of Project Management, which will provide you with a framework for the successful management of the Law of Triple Constraints. For those entering the professional services arena as a consultant, you merely need to understand that this law governs your ability to deliver to your customer's expectations. The law is real, and if you ignore it, it will certainly come back to bite you.

FIELD EXAMPLE: MISALIGNED FROM THE BEGINNING

When I first met Erich Rusch, he was an excellent lead developer who was unsure of his career path. I sensed he was ready to leave our company, as he had been clear with me that he considered himself more of a product developer than a consultant. I had always found him easy to work with, and I knew we needed him to play a central role in the rebuilding of our team, so I asked him to stick around for the experience.

He made the decision to stay long enough for us to recognize his incredible capacity for leadership in the field. Eventually, he did move on and worked with some pretty cool product development teams, but his ability to deliver customer success and abide by the principles he has adopted became legendary to the point where he found it hard to escape the lucrative demands of several of his previous customers. He now finds himself at the helm of an exciting and young consulting firm that is delivering enterprise solutions to some of the country's biggest names. Here Erich relives a situation we were both intimately involved in resolving. It is the quintessential dilemma that occurs frequently at an enterprise-sized engagement kick off -- realign now or suffer the consequences.

"One of my most difficult situations as a consultant occurred during my first project as a lead technical architect for a Software-as-a-Service (SaaS) vendor. My company sold a solution that automated a complex business process, and I was leading one of our largest engagements with one of the world's leading oncology equipment manufacturers. In preparing for the engagement kick-off, the sales team told us that the project would be under considerable budgetary pressure, so we were prepared for some difficult conversations with respect to budget and any minor enhancements they might request. As it was our first chance to clarify their desired outcome and solidify our project plan, the whole team was looking forward to the kick-off.

Prior to the kickoff, we had many internal discussions on the topic of how the customer wanted the final solution to work. During our sales process, we had

PRINCIPLE #3: MANAGE EXPECTATIONS   111

assumed that the customer wanted a solution that gave them only a handful of potential different outcomes. During the kick off however, it became obvious that the customer wanted a far more flexible solution than we had anticipated. As we gathered more data, it became clear that we were misaligned on several key assumptions regarding the difficulty required to implement the solution. While we had allowed for a considerable amount of development effort, it was clear that that our team did not have enough manpower to deliver to the customer's expectations within the given budget and timeframe.

Our team knew that we must address this misalignment as soon as possible. In our kickoff call, our project manager led the charge discussing the complexities of the desired solution and the impossibility of making this work within the given budget and timeframe. I remember sitting in the kick-off contemplating whether I should raise this issue. Was there was a way for us to complete the work within the context of the original scope? Am I really sure I know what I am talking about? Will my team support me? Will my company support me? In my heart, I wanted to find a way to make all of this possible, but it had reached a point where my mind was telling me that I had to alert everyone to what I was sure was a ticking time bomb. We were always encouraged to employ our best judgment and that the company would support us, so I decided to raise the issue.

The customer's reaction was unpleasant. From their perspective, we were derailing the project just as it was getting started. This was very alarming to them, and their frustration boiled over so much during the kick-off meeting that the situation had escalated to our senior management by the end of the day. During these conversations, the client's executive sponsor did a fair bit of venting, but my management team handled the call in a very calm and constructive manner, and they agreed to put the project on hold and escalate the issue even further to our company's CEO. Wow! My first engagement as the technical lead and, within a day, it was on hold and had escalated all the way to the CEO.

Our executives knew how to handle situations like this. They walked the tightrope between fair but firm. They were very empathetic to the customer's situation, but at the same time, we held them accountable for the information they had provided during the sales process (as this was the basis of our original estimate). Once the customer was open to investigating possible solutions to the situation, we started looking for ways to make the engagement mutually successful. The situation forced us to take a hard look at the requirements and to truly define what success looked like. We discovered that a large portion of the solution was not necessary for the initial go live; in fact, a lot of their initial requirements were nice to have and not critical or even available in today's solution!

As a result, we came up with creative solutions to share the workload, including bringing the customer's development team into the implementation team to maximize our ability to complete the requested scope. The customer agreed to increase the budget to the requisite level so as to reflect the new scope and restart the engagement. Not only was the project back on-track and the customer's expectations realigned, but we had also achieved it without wasting the customer's budget by escalating the issue immediately at the engagement kick-

off. Previously in my career, I would have been more likely to hold on to this knowledge and try and find a way to just make it happen. In this company, we were encouraged to act on our belief in the principles.

Speaking up at the engagement kick-off proved invaluable as the entire engagement team was now better positioned to deliver a successful solution, and the customer's team was in a much better position to maintain the solution after it was launched. Ultimately, the project turned out better than we could have ever expected. This customer became a huge advocate for our company, and their trust in our abilities to tell them the truth and manage their expectations successfully led to multiple follow up engagements. It was a defining engagement for my career and taught me a lot about how to manage enterprise engagements. In a small way, it is this kind of confidence in my ability to manage such situations correctly that gave me the courage to start my own professional services."

HOW DO EXPECTATIONS BECOME MISALIGNED?

During the course of an engagement, conversations are constantly taking place about a variety of topics. These numerous conversations generate emails and documentation that can expand rapidly to the point of becoming overwhelming. Despite their intention to clarify what *done* looks like, it is easy for this plethora of data to skew or confuse it! When *done* is skewed, expectations become misaligned. This can cause some of the engagement team to be heading towards one version of *done* while others head in the direction of a different version. It only takes a slight misalignment to split an otherwise united engagement team, and hence, begin the process of veering the engagement away from a successful conclusion. This section will explore the two most common ways in which expectations can become misaligned and how you can learn to reduce their impact on your engagement's outcome.

Leaving Expectation Gaps

Expectations have the potential to become misaligned when we create them and leave out important details. If we leave out necessary details about an expectation, it creates an information gap that will eventually be filled with or without our input. This is known as an *Expectation Gap*. When such a gap exists, the customer will fill it by selecting one of a number of potential approaches. Unfortunately, you face the problem of uncertainty as to which approach the customer will employ, which can easily misalign even the most basic of expectations. The list below details the four most common approaches a customer may employ to fill in the missing detail. For the purpose of illustrating the effect of each approach, let's say you told a customer that *the project plan would be sent to them on Friday*, and you provided no further details.

Method	Description
Experience	In some instances, the customer's historical experience with such circumstances will fill in the missing details. If previous service providers delivered project plans or other deliverables at the beginning of the working day, then the expectation may be that it will arrive by 9:00am Friday morning. If you do not send it by that time, your customer may be asking for it as soon as that time passes.
Desire	In some instances, the customer will complete the omitted details by using his or her desire to be successful. Even though you may not have been notified of the need, your customer may expect you to meet their desired timeline. For example, if the customer has a meeting with the executive stakeholders at 2:00pm on Friday, he or she may expect the

	plan to be sent before that time. It may be assumed that you know the importance of having the plan available for that meeting, so the desire to be ready for it may drive the expectation.
Trust	In this instance, the details that you have omitted from an expectation may be filled by the degree of trust the customer has in you. If he or she trusts you, then you may not be asked for them until the following day. This is still a very dangerous situation because neither of you really knows what the other is thinking. You may still be thinking that the project plan is due at 3:00pm on Friday, but the customer may trust that you will have it to them by 10:00am.
Request	Sometimes the customer may recognize that you have left out some details, and he or she may reach out to you to supply them. This is rare, but smart customers are good at managing their service providers, and they may recognize (as should you) that the ambiguity exists and must be resolved. They may take the proactive step of asking you to address the expectation gap. If this happens too often, you are going to look as if you do not know how to set expectations correctly. You do not want your customer thinking that they need to help set and manage expectations. If they do, then they will feel as though they are doing the work that you should be doing.

Not only are there numerous ways to fill expectation gaps, but a customer may also fill a gap by using more than one of the available options. Unfortunately, this has the potential to create erratic results, which is precisely the type of unpredictability you're trying to remove from your engagements. It is difficult to hold yourself to perfection in this matter because expectations are being set (and re-set) all the time, but you must remain vigilant and be able to recognize those moments. As a way to trigger yourself into action, it is helpful to remember that the most important expectations typically relate to the triple constraints. So you should take notice of any discussion pertaining to scope, effort, time, and quality, as they are likely to be linked with the setting of an expectation.

Implicit Acceptance of Expectations

Another way that expectations become misaligned is when the customer makes a false assumption or statement that the service provider's team fails to correct. Unfortunately, in this circumstance, silence is tantamount to acceptance of the false statement. If a customer indicates that he expects you'll deliver a document by Wednesday, and you believe that it will be delivered on Thursday, you *must* speak up! The momentary conflict you will create is far better than the one that will follow if you let the chance to correct the misalignment slip. It is all too easy for us to claim that we would *always* speak up in these circumstances. The reality is that it is harder than we think to stop the momentum of the meeting and address the conflict.

I have witnessed too many instances in which the customer was allowed to believe that an incorrect assumption was true. The problem arises because individual consultants fear that stepping into the spotlight and raising the concern might ruffle some feathers, and so they assume this uncomfortable task is not their job. While this sentiment is understandable, you should be aware that your silence creates what is referred to as an *implicit acceptance* of the incorrect statement. By refusing to correct a mistaken belief, the customer simply takes your silence as acceptance of it. You have but a moment to correct an incorrect statement. If you do not, then you are witnessing the point at which your expectation becomes misaligned.

Many professional services consultants expect a customer to self-validate an expectation. By this, I mean that they expect the customer to know when their own expectation is unachievable or misaligned. While many customers make an earnest effort to have realistic expectations, they do not possess your level of skill and knowledge. Hence, it is possible that they may believe that some things are possible when they are not. You must remember that *you* are the expert. As the expert, they are relying on your ability to guide them to realistic and achievable expectations while delivering on your commitment to customer success.

When I perform a post-mortem or "lessons learned" session on an engagement that has suffered this fate, I ask my team, "Did you ever think of saying something to reset this expectation?" Unfortunately, the response is often, "No, we just assumed the customer knew that it was unrealistic." Simply put, customers are depending on you to tell them what is and isn't possible. You are being paid to deliver the best solution possible, so the customer may not know when a request becomes impossible. If you fail to object to an impossible request, the customer will assume that you have agreed to it.

After you have implicitly agreed to a false statement, it is very hard to reset that expectation later. In the customer's mind, if the request had not been possible, then you would have objected to it at the time that it had been made. The customer may begin to assume your inability to speak up about the misalignment indicates that you're not sufficiently trustworthy to guide them to success. The customer may also try to pressure you into delivering on the unrealistic expectation because the customer's stakeholders or executives are now unwilling to accept any outcome other than the one you led them to believe was possible.

Looking at it from their perspective, why should they reset their expectation when you gave them every reason to believe it was going to happen? In this respect, implicit expectations are very dangerous, and they can quickly arise if you miss your window of opportunity to speak up. Even if you do miss the initial window, it is always worth interrupting the subsequent conversations to go back and address it. So, don't sit there and stew on a missed opportunity; speak up! We will discuss tactics for successfully achieving this in Principle #4: Having Difficult Conversations Early.

FIELD EXAMPLE: TICK-TICK-TICK-BOOM!

To illustrate the immense danger of misaligned expectations, I will recount an experience I had during a difficult engagement. In this example, we were building a complex system for a very traditional business that had a very small IT team. The customer's team was comprised of jacks-of-all-trades rather than experts in a particular domain. We were their first Software as a Service (SaaS) vendor, and we had been struggling to simplify their complex business processes that had been developed in the age of paper forms and rubber stamps. Our final solution had been up and running for months, but issues were arising weekly with regard to some inconsistencies in terms of how our software was performing a specific set of calculations.

One morning, I arrived at work to attend an escalation meeting via conference call with their Chief Information Officer (CIO), the engagement's executive sponsor. Due to the on-going issues, the CEO and Head of Sales were internally pressuring him to resolve the situation, and he wanted answers. As a side note, you can't even imagine the pressure being placed on this person. He had committed $500,000 of the company's money to invest in software that would drastically improve his global company's operations. From his perspective, this was more than a failing investment. The solution we had implemented was making it harder for them to carry out their day-to-day business and had effectively made their business environment worse! Having been in a similar position to those of the CIO, I knew perfectly well how it felt: it is uncomfortable, and you feel as though the weight of the world is coming down on you. If you do not resolve the situation quickly, you will be out of a job.

"The system is not displaying our data accurately," complained the CIO. "We've paid good money for this solution, and we have nothing to show for it!" his voice was already agitated, and I could feel his anger rising through the telephone.

This was not a new observation as there had been repeated instances of accurate data calculations suddenly becoming incorrect. This escalation related to such an occasion. We requested more details about the issue they were currently facing, and then we analyzed it. As we were analyzing this detail, one of my team members pointed out that we had agreed the acceptance criteria for this scenario three months prior, and that it had passed that test shortly afterward. We even showed them the data we had used to test that calculation, and the confirmation from their own team that it had been done satisfactorily.

The customer's senior operations person chimed in, "Yes we agreed to that formula, but our way of calculating this data has changed."

With a raised eyebrow I probed "Are you saying that your issue is that we correctly implemented the data calculation, but you have since changed how you want it to work?"

"Yes" the customer replied. "You are software as a service are you not? We are expecting you to continue to service our business and ensure that our rules are always kept up to date."

If you are not in the software industry then you may have missed the "gotcha" in this conversation. It is subtle but significant. When selling Software-as-a-Service, the "Service" is providing the software itself, not the on-going maintenance of the logic or business rules within it. Although we may be willing to provide such an on-going service, we call that type of business; outsourcing or a managed service. In such circumstances, the customer pays someone to operate or manage a part of its business on their behalf.

It is easy to see where a company inexperienced with Software-as-a-Service vendors might believe that an on-going maintenance "service" was included in the service they purchased. SaaS providers sell software that is accessible over the Internet, and the customer continues to pay a subscription fee for access to the software. While a SaaS company will guide its customer on how to use the software it sells, the business logic that gets implemented must remain the decision of the customer otherwise they are not in control of the performance of their own business. SaaS companies often offer an additional service to assist the customer in administering their own data but it is never a part of the basic software service.

Unfortunately, there was a misaligned expectation in the type of "service" we were providing. The customer believed it included the on-going maintenance of their business logic. Although this confusion was easy to clarify, the expectations gap led the customer to expect something well beyond the service we were contracted to provide. Although we provided the software through which the data calculations took place, it was still their responsibility to maintain the calculations their day-to-day business relied upon. The only way to resolve the situation was for the customer to pay for the unanticipated cost of hiring someone to perform this on-going function, which put the CIO in a precarious position. This additional ongoing cost was never budgeted for, and now he needed to go back and ask for more money from the company CFO.

This ticking time bomb was about to go off, and the CIO vented his frustration. Although I can't be certain this was the final straw, he did not remain in that position long thereafter. I mention this because it illustrates that in most misalignment situations, the customer's executive sponsor can suffer a far greater consequences than you. Because of this, you must do everything you can to prevent these misalignments. It is easy for both sides in this example to point fingers at each other, but to be a great service provider you must take it upon yourself to make expectations as clear as possible. In hindsight, my team should have had a better hand over process to the customer and made sure that they understood the operational requirements the customer was expected to own before going live with the system.

The customer pays a far greater price than you for a failed engagement. You go back to your firm a little worse for wear and get assigned to another engagement. Life goes on. Your customer's stakeholders are stuck with a big "F" on their

foreheads and will live in fear that their days are numbered, and in some instances, they are.

This example demonstrates how a misaligned expectation can float silently within an engagement undetected, ultimately exploding like a bomb, even *after* the engagement was completed. This issue lurked beneath the surface through the sales and implementation process without being discovered, and then *boom!* The misaligned expectation explodes over someone's career. Misaligned expectations are incredibly dangerous to an engagement and to your customer. They are not always visible, so you must stay alert and not only identify them, but also disarm them immediately.

WHO, WHAT, WHEN AND THE THREE HOWS

Whenever you make a commitment to a customer, it sets an expectation. As that commitment could be for such a wide variety of things, it's almost impossible to validate that every expectation has been correctly set. However, if you remain alert, there is a method for ensuring that you have covered the basics. So long as you employ this process, only the most obscure expectations have a potential to be misaligned. Therefore, you should adopt the following method but always keep your antenna up for an expectation that may prove to be the exception.

A typical professional services expectation has six primary attributes. I refer to them as *Who, What, When and the Three Hows*. For each of the attributes, it is important to be as specific as possible. For example, to correctly set an expectation about *when* something will happen, be very specific about the time, which means specifying the date, the time and the time zone.

To illustrate how these attributes need to be applied, let's revisit the example of setting the expectation of providing the customer with a project plan on Friday with no other information provided.

Who

Refers to who is responsible and accountable for delivering upon the expectation. In this example, we will name the specific person in charge of the project plan Mary M., the service provider's project manager. She is both responsible for delivering the project plan and accountable for the quality of it. However, the term *who* also refers to the people to whom the deliverable will be distributed. By forgetting to include someone in the distribution of information, expectations can easily be misaligned. Therefore, it is critical to keep *everyone* who is relevant to the situation in the loop. In this example, the project plan must be provided to the project stakeholders (Audrey N., Tess C., James P., and Kylee J.), and the customer's project manager (Mat E.).

There is a very good industry acronym known as RACI that helps you remember the important types of *Who* that you should consider. RACI stands for Responsible, Accountable, Consulted, and Informed and it describes the four different roles that people can play in delivering to an expectation. Remembering this acronym can help you set expectations with greater clarity.

What

Refers to the "something" that is going to be expected. In this example the "something" is a project plan. Being specific, however, Mary will only be providing the first draft of the Phase

1 project plan. Until now, the customer may have assumed that the *project plan* was going to be for the both Phase 1 and Phase 2.

When

Refers to the time and date when the expectation will be fulfilled. In our example, the deadline is cited as next Friday but the intent was to mean the Friday after that, being Friday, February 7[th]at 3:00pm EDT (remember to be specific about time and time zone). Failing to specify the exact time and date is a common cause of misaligned expectations.

How Well?

Refers to the level of quality the expectation will be delivered to. Mary is intending on delivering the first *draft* version of the project plan for feedback. If she omitted this detail, the customer may have assumed this was the *final* project plan.

How Will it be Delivered?

What process will be deployed to deliver the expectation? In a lot of circumstances, how something gets delivered is critical to what to expect once it is delivered. In this example, Mary is only receiving input from the service provider's team; hence, the project plan will not be aligned with any of the customer's other plans. It is expected that the plan will be presented as a first draft at a meeting with the customer, the attendees of which will come from the *who* definition above. At this meeting, Mary is expecting to gather the customer's input and align it with their plan. Without fully understanding this, the customer may arrive at the meeting upset that the plan was being presented without including their input.

How Much?

Refers to the cost required or the price to be paid in order for the expectation to be delivered. In this example, the customer has paid in advance for Mary and her team's hours. If the plan originally included these hours for planning purposes, then the cost is already incorporated into the original engagement price. However, if they were not then Mary must determine how the unexpected effort is going to be accounted for.

Everything you do on a services engagement has an estimated cost associated to it, so you must ensure that you know if that cost is being funded, and exactly how many hours you have to apply to it. When in doubt, you should always ask your engagement's project manager.

Who, what, when and the *three how(s)* is a simple way to remember the important questions relevant to setting expectations during an engagement. It is an effective reminder of the details necessary to ensure that expectations are clearly set.

THE IMPORTANCE OF ESTIMATES

Whenever a customer asks the following questions, the answer you provide is actually providing an estimate.

- How much time will it take?

- How many people do you need to make that happen?

- How much will it cost?

- How difficult is that to do?

As we have discussed, the business of professional services is won or lost on estimates. Estimates can make or break an engagement, so you must be attuned to the precise moment at which an estimate is setting an expectation with your customer. Hence, it is important to remember that "off the cuff" answers to questions such as these are thoroughly discouraged.

During an engagement, a consultant should NEVER provide a customer with an unapproved estimate. Estimates must be validated by peer review, and your engagement manager must formally provide them to your customer.

Your engagement manager will, however, ask you to estimate the effort remaining to complete your assigned activities. It is critical that you understand the importance of accurately reporting this information. This is because your engagement has a very defined plan that aims to achieve its goals and objectives through the exertion of a very specific amount of effort. Any variance to this planned accumulation of value from effort is incredibly important to the people in charge of managing your engagement's budget. Engagement managers typically need to know three very important attributes of the task you are trying to complete.

- The hours of effort you have put into the task (commonly known as *Effort Consumed* or *Hours Logged*)

- The progress you have made towards completing the task (commonly known as *Percent Complete*)

- The remaining hours required to complete the task (commonly known as *Estimate to Complete* or *Effort Remaining*)

These three values assist engagement managers in evaluating if a project is on track to deliver its promised outcomes within the original constraints placed upon it by the contract (time, effort, price). Your entire team will be asked to report these metrics so that they can be fed into a much larger project management process. As any engagement manager will tell you, it can be the simplest of tasks that can send an engagement off the tracks by consuming far more hours than originally estimated. The purpose of this section is not to bore you with project management detail. However, I must impress upon you the importance of adhering to the estimates that govern the time you can apply to any task, as well as the critical need for you to accurately estimate the effort remaining to complete that task. Without maintaining accurate time data and estimates, it is unlikely that your engagement is able to determine exactly when and where it will finish.

CHAPTER SUMMARY

A great service provider understands the expectations inherent in an engagement. They recognize the setting of expectations, and they can identify when and how well expectations are being set. If a great service provider spots an expectation that is unachievable, he or she will act quickly to realign it.

Your customers do not want to fail, nor do they want you to fail. Their jobs are on the line and their desired outcome is in your hands. This creates a lot of anxiety and you need to bring your "A" game every day to make sure that expectations are correctly aligned so that you can all be successful.

Your customers are financially constrained, and sometimes they will want far more than you can provide them. It is their job to get the most value from you while paying as little as possible. They will always push for you to achieve more in a shorter timeframe and for less money. However, it is your responsibility to manage their expectations such that these financial constraints work profitably for your firm. To do this, you must accurately set expectations and properly maintain them throughout the entire engagement.

Just like the tightrope walker, you cannot attempt a feat that is beyond your capability; yet at the same time, your crowd wants a spectacle worth paying for. Set the expectation too low and the customer will wonder why they even have you there; set it too high and you are likely to overcommit and disappoint them. A lackadaisical approach to aligning expectations puts hope in charge of your safety as you cross the tightrope. You might get lucky once, but at some point you will certainly fall. A rigorous approach to managing expectations is critical to maintaining balance as you cross your tightrope successfully.

HAVE DIFFICULT CONVERSATIONS EARLY

"Disciplining yourself to do what you know is right and important, although difficult, is the highroad to pride, self-esteem, and personal satisfaction."

– Margaret Thatcher

STEP UP TO THE PLATE

As the previous chapter describes, expectations can easily become misaligned. Once you've identified a misalignment, you must take action. This principle focuses on the appropriate manner for taking such action, and it provides tips and techniques for doing so effectively. Conversations to realign expectations are difficult because one or both of you are going to have to accept a different, perhaps less optimal, outcome than what you are currently expecting. Yet, without addressing these misalignments, your engagement is doomed. The principle of *Having Difficult Conversations Early* is designed to help you recognize their dire importance and motivate you to act on situations that require them immediately, regardless of how difficult they may be.

If we return again to our image of the tightrope walker, we will recognize that any person who performs a dangerous activity will also surround himself with experts and advisors. Someone engaged in dangerous activity will seek the counsel and wisdom of people they trust prior to taking a new risk. As safety in these circumstances is paramount, these daredevils employ advisors who they trust will always bring an issue to their attention even if that conversation will be difficult. The performer trusts their advisors to scrutinize every facet of the activity and speak up the moment they identify something they feel may jeopardize safety. Even if he is otherwise blind to the risk and stubbornly walking into danger, the performer trusts that his advisors will not be afraid to speak the plain awful truth to him and get his attention if needed.

Consider Felix Baumgartner, who performed the death-defying feat of his record-breaking Red Bull Stratos skydive in October, 2012. In preparation to skydive solo from the stratosphere, he employed seven trusted advisors to help him prepare and maximize his chances of a safe jump. These seven people also managed many other people, who analyzed endless amounts of data, reviewing safety concepts and designs focused on making their specific part of the jump a success. But with so much work being done across so many different areas, Mr. Baumgartner trusted his safety to just a small team of seven advisors. He entrusted them to analyze the feat alongside him and ensure that it was technically possible and as safe as possible. He was so sure of it that he was betting his life that they would have the necessary difficult conversations with him as soon as anything looked unsafe. He counted on them to help strike the balance between breaking the world record in a death-defying leap while also stopping the feat from becoming too dangerous.

Once again, we can be grateful that our job doesn't carry the same consequences of failure, but your job has similar characteristics to that of Mr. Baumgartner's advisors. Your customer is up on his or her own tightrope, and he or she is taking risks. You must step up to the plate and mitigate these risks. You must find a way to get your customer to the other side of their tightrope. After all, you're the services tightrope-walking expert. You walk the services tightrope for a living, and you do nothing but help customers successfully walk their own tightropes time and time again. This means that it is your responsibility to identify dangers that may jeopardize your customer's success, and it is your job to act urgently when something is amiss.

More specifically, when you notice something problematic, you should promptly engage in the necessary conversation required to address it. Although these conversations are difficult, they are highly beneficial in that they are also the greatest moments for you to prove your value to the customer. These conversations are difficult for a reason – someone is going to be disappointed or potentially angry as a result of it. This is always an uncomfortable feeling for the person who has the difficult news to announce. The impending emotional eruption and ire is understandably terrifying. But you must convince yourself that proactive and controlled action now is far better than uncontrollable reaction later. I have often thought that it is only the most outstanding consultants that have the courage to attack these conversations, so I challenge you to strive toward that level of excellence. Despite the adversity you'll face, instances like these provide you with the greatest opportunity to become the customer's trusted advisor.

THE COST OF DOING NOTHING

Professional services engagements often fail because someone failed to act with sufficient urgency to avoid the consequences of an issue once it was spotted. While we would all like to tell ourselves that we would always take quick and timely action, the reality is that we often avoid or delay a difficult conversation simply because it is uncomfortable. It is in our nature to not want to be in a situation that makes us uneasy. Unfortunately for a professional services consultant, this natural reaction is the antithesis of what a trusted advisor should do for his or her customer.

In my opinion, a consultant's true worth is measured by the speed at which issues are brought to the customer's attention regardless of who is at fault, or the difficulty of the conversation.

An engagement is a series of chained events, and hence, the outcome of each engagement activity creates the foundation for the next. This chain reaction of events means that the misaligned expectation becomes the foundation for new outcomes. If the misalignment is not corrected then that new outcome may also become further misaligned. This chain reaction continues until the misalignment is found. Once it is discovered, not only does the original misalignment need correcting, but so too may every subsequent outcome that relied upon it. Hence, the cost of doing nothing about a misalignment becomes exponentially worse the longer it exists.

To be a great professional services consultant, this truth must disturb you. You must see these kinds of misalignments as a virus that threatens your engagement's very existence. Your dedication to identifying, analyzing, and killing the virus must pale in comparison to the awkwardness of having to discuss it with your customer. You cannot avoid the natural and uncomfortable feeling that the matter may best be dealt with *later*, so instead you need a stronger emotion such as an overwhelming belief that you must take action *immediately*.

This chapter hopes to light a fire under all of us by underscoring the necessity that we must be passionate about attacking *important* problems *at the moment we discover them!* Nothing is more frustrating to a manager or a customer who, after discovering the misaligned expectation for themselves, also finds out that several people on the engagement team were aware of it all along.

When you notice a misaligned expectation, act swiftly as the cost of resolving it will only continue to increase.

Time may heal all wounds, but for engagement misalignments, it only serves to make them more expensive. To further illustrate the damage caused by these misaligned expectations, I have listed a short description of the two types of costs you are likely to incur as misalignments age.

Direct Costs: The Cost to Fix the Misalignment
The direct costs that you suffer from failing to have difficult conversations early, are those that you must financially incur to resolve the misalignment. This creates a cost blowout that can best be illustrated with a real world example. If a construction crew mixed a poor batch of concrete for a house's foundation but did not notice it, then the foundation will set improperly. It may dry hard as a rock, but it may have a tendency to become prematurely weak. The consequences of this flaw now become an issue for the rest of the construction work. While the mistake remains undetected, every subsequent

step of the construction unintentionally inherits its consequences.

The wood frame is then built and secured to a foundation that will not last. The wiring is then secured to the wooden frame. The cost to resolve the faulty foundation now includes the direct cost to fix the wood frame and the wiring. The wiring and then the framing will need to be removed so that the foundation can get fixed and rebuilt. All of this work adds to the total cost to fix the issue and increases it beyond what it would have been if the issues with the foundation's mix were addressed when it was poured.

The total cost to fix the issues includes the cost to tear down the existing structures and then rebuild them all again. These are all direct costs because someone is going to have to pay for that work. In construction, much like in professional services, it is usually the firm providing the service that will bear the largest portion of these costs. This is because the customer will argue that it is the responsibility of a high quality service provider to not make such mistakes. The reality is that this is a hard argument to rebuff without causing some damage to your status as a trusted advisor. It is these kinds of situations that you must try and avoid at all costs. You can negotiate your way out of it and force the customer to agree to pay for some of the direct costs to fix the misalignment, but it will surely leave a bitter taste in their mouth.

Just like construction projects, professional services engagements are rarely a collection of unrelated activities. From the moment the sales teams begins selling, through to the final acceptance, the outcome from each activity becomes an input for the next. If any of these activities become misaligned, then your engagement will start to veer in the wrong direction and the direct cost of fixing it will grow with each subsequent step.

Failure to have the necessary difficult conversations to address this misdirection is only making the final costs to correct it more expensive.

Indirect Costs: The Cost to Your Reputation

By the same token, some costs exceed the simplicity of dollars and cents. Perhaps the biggest cost of doing nothing is the cost to your reputation as a trusted advisor. On a critical issue, the customer may consider your inaction a violation of the trust you had set out to obtain. If you cannot be trusted to have a difficult conversation in a timely manner, then surely you are not providing the kind of service that the customer can rely upon in the future. In repairing ailing services teams, I have seen firsthand the true cost of this failure. A reputation for unreliable action can spread industry-wide rather quickly, and a services firm's reputation can be adversely impacted. I have witnessed the painful efforts required to reverse this trend, both within an existing customer and within the industry, and it is incredibly difficult to achieve. Not only had our mistakes created direct costs to repair them, but we also accrued the indirect costs of customers going elsewhere for their future business.

The cost of doing nothing has an extraordinary impact on a professional services organization's reputation and profitability. You must take action as soon as you spot a misaligned expectation, and you must have that difficult conversation to begin addressing it as soon as possible. These misalignments are like ticking time bombs. From the moment you notice it you must act. You should *always* discuss it with your manager first, but you must get the bomb-squad assembled as soon as possible. Be aware that you must try and defuse it before it becomes hidden within other engagement outcomes. This single misalignment is staring you in the face. Act now before it is too late.

THE DISTRACTION OF URGENCY

Apart from the awkwardness of having difficult conversations, there is another key reason why professional consultants tend not to act in a timely manner. While the situation occurs frequently, I have seen the reason for it remain invisible to the professional services manager and the consultant alike. This other reason is best expressed by Dwight D. Eisenhower's famous quote, *"What is important is seldom urgent and what is urgent is seldom important."*

To effectively determine which difficult conversations are worth having, you must determine their importance. Important matters are those that will truly affect the outcome of the engagement. Unimportant matters may affect a part of the engagement, but they ultimately will not impact whether or not the engagement will be deemed a success. It is very common for unimportant matters to be *dressed up* as important by simply placing a great deal of urgency on them. The urgency compels us to act on the matter regardless of its level of importance. This false sense of importance can hence distract our attention, and we can find ourselves wasting valuable time chasing down issues of little importance (because they are urgent) while important issues (that are not yet urgent) go unresolved.

Complex professional services engagements are full of such urgent issues. Amidst the flurry of urgent requests there is a mix of both important and not so important issues. The urgent, but not important issues, are often smaller and actionable so professional services consultants and customers can be drawn toward them because the sense of accomplishment is easier to attain. They create a feeling of accomplishment while holding the dread of addressing the bigger issues at bay. Sometimes, however, we can get so consumed by the unimportant urgent matters that we may not even be aware of the engagement's important ones. Resolving the urgent but unimportant issues is like eating junk food. While it tastes great, it is full of empty calories. Eventually, you are going to need to eat something more substantive. For an engagement to be well nourished, someone must track down and devour the important issues.

It takes a well-trained eye to sift through the list of urgent issues and filter out the less important ones. It takes an ever better eye to look through the list of urgent but unimportant issues and elevate the important ones that lay just behind them so that they can be resolved before they become urgent. So before you decide to have that difficult conversation, think to yourself, "Am I truly chasing down an important issue, or am I wasting time chasing down an unimportant urgent issue?" You can often be surprised by the clarity this simple question can bring.

In an environment full of distractions, the value of focusing on the important and urgent, at the expense of the urgent and unimportant cannot be understated. The success of an engagement is not measured by how well it handles urgent matters, but by how well it filters out the unimportant matters so that it can identify and act on those that are truly important.

IS IT MY JOB TO HAVE DIFFICULT CONVERSATIONS?

YES! One of this chapter's major themes is that it is *everyone's* job to identify and act on misaligned expectations. Every professional services executive has had far too many conversations with people who failed to identify that it was their responsibility to speak up about a problem they witnessed. It is difficult to teach individuals to act with a sense of urgency about important matters, but I have focused on this principle with every team I've ever managed, and it is possible to make great improvements quickly. Any team that desires to be a high quality service provider must adopt this principle passionately and uniformly. In such a circumstance, each individual should ask himself or herself, "What am I waiting for? Take action!"

For a professional services team to succeed, everyone in the team must be committed to watching out for the little things that require realignment, and they must be prepared to speak up appropriately. As with any team-based activity, each member of a service delivery team has his or her own areas of responsibility. This means that it is the role of the individual within an engagement or professional services firm to dictate the level of action that he or she can take once a misalignment is identified. Such factors may include: the timing of the discovery, the experience level and seniority of the individual who discovered it, and the seniority of the customer's representative whose expectation is misaligned.

However, this does not preclude someone from taking action on a misalignment that is witnessed outside of his or her area of expertise or control. I firmly recommend that *every* professional services consultant be authorized to bring attention to *any* misalignment they witness. The key is making sure that each consultant understands how to discern the correct action to take in a given circumstance as to avoid creating an unnecessary customer escalation.

For this reason, let's review the techniques available for you in such situations. These approaches provide a range of actions that you can select based upon the level of attention you feel that you are authorized to bring to a misalignment. Selecting the correct approach means that the customer is aware of the issue and joins you in resolving it. Selecting the incorrect approach can cause an escalation that has you and the customer taking sides and defending their positions. The difference is a cooperative environment for realigning the issue versus a combative one.

Proactive Escalation

The best kind of difficult conversation is the one that you control entirely. If you happen to identify a misaligned expectation that the customer is unaware of, then it is often very effective to deploy what I call a *Proactive Escalation.*

A proactive escalation is where the service provider identifies the issue and escalates it directly to the customer with a preferred recommendation on how to resolve it before the customer has a chance to identify that the issue exists. This is *proactive* because most escalations are *reactive* once the customer has identified that what you delivered did not meet with what they were expecting. In this instance, you turn the tables on the process and, by preparing in advance, you create an opportunity to realign the expectation successfully and prove yourself as a trusted advisor.

Speaking up about the misalignment before the customer has identified it has the following advantages:

- The customer may be upset about the situation, but he or she is unlikely to be sufficiently prepared to go on the offensive.

- The service provider can propose the preferred resolution to the issue immediately. This helps resolve the issue faster and prevents the need for the customer to be requesting a range of resolutions that are not possible (which only serves to waste engagement resources).

- Even if the customer is irked by the situation, he will appreciate the proactive approach because it demonstrates that the service provider puts the customer's success above the difficulty of speaking up. This is the characteristic of a truly a trusted advisor.

All of these points work in your favor when compared with a customer bringing an issue that they have discovered directly to you. When a customer escalates the issue to you, they will be on the offensive. They will already have thought of numerous ways they would like the issue resolved, and they will be disappointed that you were not able to spot it sooner. Hence, it is going to cost more to resolve it reactively than to resolve it proactively.

Correct the Misalignment

If the customer is already aware of the misalignment, then you may decide to hit this problem head-on and immediately begin to realign the expectation. Be careful. You may be walking into a heated discussion that will come back on you. Later in this chapter, we are going to discuss a process for conducting such conversations called *Empathy, Understanding, and Resolution,* and it is a three-step process focused on guiding difficult conversations towards a successful outcome.

While we will detail this process later, if you are going to try and realign a customer expectation with it, then you must remember this key rule.

Only realign expectations that you are responsible for delivering.

This means that while you should highlight misaligned expectations as soon as you identify them, you shouldn't attempt to realign matters that are not a part of your direct responsibility.

If you do, it is unlikely that you will be able to execute a successful resolution. These moments call for detailed knowledge of the subject matter for which the expectation was misaligned. If you have it, then realign it, if you do not, then plan to take the next best action and *plant the seed*.

Plant the Seed

If you are not going to address the issue directly, then it is still important that you say something. As I have already said, silence is regarded as implicit agreement, so I recommend that at a minimum you plant the seed of doubt about the alignment of the expectation. When faced with the need to speak in a potentially explosive situation, this is a good alternative to trying to realign the expectation then and there. If you think that you may not have the authority to correct the misalignment and begin the resolution process, then you may want to plant the seed of doubt by saying something like this.

"That is interesting. I am not 100% sure that is correct. I need to do a little more research, so can we table this until I've looked into it further? I do not think we should proceed under the assumption that this is correct until I have confirmed it."

This approach raises the flag immediately, and it puts your audience on notice of the issue. However, it also does not indicate the degree to which you think the expectation is misaligned. You may think that the customer's expectation is entirely wrong, but this approach allows you to plant the seed that a misalignment exists without mentioning its severity.

Once again, it becomes critical that you meet with your own team as soon as you exit this meeting. Your seed of doubt won't last long, and you will need your team's help to clarify the situation as soon as possible. You may have temporarily halted the proliferation of the misalignment, but you do not know for how long. It is still your responsibility to notify your manager immediately so that the misalignment can be corrected.

Say Nothing, but Escalate Internally Immediately

I cannot recommend that you take this approach, however, I do understand that some people may believe they are unable to tactfully speak up in a given situation. If you do decide to hold your tongue, then you must understand that you are responsible to escalate to your manager immediately after the customer interaction. By holding your tongue, you are providing implicit acceptance of the misalignment, and hence, you have allowed the expectation time bomb to start ticking. While it pains me to include this option, I can see that in some rare circumstances it may be the only choice a consultant can safely take. This option is so dangerous because once that time bombs starts ticking, it may only take a moment for it to drift further into the customer's organization, thus making it that much harder to eventually find and defuse.

Selecting an Approach

Please take care in selecting your approach. This is one of the most difficult tightropes to walk, and it can become perilous very quickly despite a promising beginning. The best recommendation is to be proactive in the approach you take provided that you are knowledgeable and responsible for the subject matter at hand. When delivering difficult news, you must be prepared for your customer to react in such a way that you may have never seen. This is perfectly normal and you cannot reciprocate the level of emotion that he or she is about to display. You must have faith that the actions you are taking will produce the best possible result in a bad situation. If you play your cards right, you will keep the customer calm and focused on the solution you propose, and you'll reinforce your status as the trusted advisor. The sooner you can have these difficult conversations, the sooner you can begin working towards the solution.

GETTING YOUR HEAD RIGHT

Regardless of how hard you try, misaligned expectations will *always* arise, and you'll need to realign them promptly. Realigning expectations is difficult because it requires that you tell the customer that they will not receive exactly what they wanted. By way of analogy, if you ordered a BMW, and you went to pick it up, you'd be disappointed if you got something less. Even if you received something of equal value, you'd still be disappointed the minute you saw it wasn't what you were expecting. While this may seem like an extreme analogy, I can guarantee you that your customer is expecting that you are the metaphorical BMW of professional services. They just put their career on the line by hiring you. They have probably already told their organization that they went and hired the best people for the job. Now that you want to realign expectations, your customer is not going to enjoy having to announce that the expectations they had set are incorrect. Nobody wants to tell their executive stakeholders that the business improvements they received funding for are now going to be less than originally promised. It can put the entire funding of the engagement at risk, not to mention the career of the person responsible for the engagement.

Due to the fear of having to go back and lower or change an existing expectation, you can expect your customer to hold on to the original expectation as long as possible. The customer may fight vehemently to have you agree to deliver the service that was originally expected. For this reason you must expect that this conversation can potentially become heated. There is a lot riding on this for the customer. The person you are negotiating with is likely to have been given the order to find a way to make this work by having you deliver a resolution as close as possible to the original expectation. In some instances, they will have been told not to negotiate at all and just force you to agree to deliver it regardless of how impossible that may be.

In these conversations, it is important that you do not make the situation worse. In a difficult conversation where your customer gets emotional and starts to accuse you of not delivering a quality service, it is easy to get defensive. It is easy to become equally emotional and verbally retaliate. While understandable, this is not going to help you resolve the issue and continue towards achieving a successful outcome. To assist you in these moments, here are two effective pieces of advice to place you in the right frame of mind for the conversation.

Remain Calm & Constructive

What's done is done. In situations like this, you must be able to compartmentalize your emotions and focus your energy on moving forward. Nobody likes to deliver bad news, but once it is delivered, a great service provider is able to focus all of his or her attention on the constructive path forward. We all have 20/20 hindsight, so there is no award for being able to pinpoint whose fault it was after the event. While it is important that a service provider be clear about the origins of an issue, it is equally important not to waste time dwelling on unconstructive recriminations and finger pointing. When in this situation, remember to repeat those two words: *Calm & Constructive.*

We make our best decisions when we are calm. Even when under pressure, if we manage to remain calm and think clearly, our decisions will be as well informed as they can be, which maximizes our chances of being constructive. Losing your cool can divert your energies into unconstructive banter or nitpicking over irrelevant issues, and that is a sure fire way to lose your reputation as a trusted advisor. A master at professional services delivery will always stay calm. Focus on the big picture. You are not being paid for brilliant hindsight; you are being paid for your ability to achieve results by pressing forward.

Some customers will use your mistakes (whether real or perceived) as a way to ratchet up the pressure on you in the hope of leveraging something more from you (free hours, reduced rates, harder work, better work). Your customer is being paid to get the most value from you for the least cost, so this is a perfectly reasonable tactic. Regardless of their efforts, you must still remain calm and have confidence in your training and your ability to make informed decisions. As a customer to other service providers, I have used this tactic and received fantastic discounts. It works really well, so be careful. However, remember our important rules like the triple constraints, and recall that in an engagement reliant upon two-way communication, it is rare that the misalignment is entirely the fault of only one team. Try and find the middle ground, and if you cannot, then offer to continue the conversation at another time. This will give you additional time to escalate it further within your team and devise another approach.

Avoid putting yourself under further pressure by answering questions you're unsure of. I have fallen into this trap, and it feels awful. I have said things like "that doesn't sound too hard, we can probably do that by Wednesday," and then the questions start to run through my mind. Maybe it is more complex than I think it is. Maybe I should have asked our project manager? Maybe it can't be done by Wednesday? As soon as you walk yourself into this situation, you'll know that you have compounded the problem by setting yet another expectation that you're unsure you can meet. This kind of mistake only increases the pressure you're under. It is OK to undo this expectation within the first few seconds after saying it. "You know what, on second thought, let me confirm what I have just said with my team, I'd hate to set the wrong expectation." This kind of admission is perfectly reasonable, and it could save you from making the situation worse.

Of course it is even better to avoid answering any question you are not sure of. After almost twenty years in professional services, one thing that I have learned is that it is OK to not have all of the answers immediately. Stay calm, take any question that you can't answer on notice, and tell the customer that you will look into it after the meeting. Even if the customer is demanding an answer immediately, I guarantee you it is better to ask for the time to get the answer right than to further compound the problem by setting the wrong expectation.

Remaining calm and proceeding through a difficult conversation in a poised manner demonstrates that you are a champion at the professional services game, and it indicates to your customer that you are an asset no matter who is at fault. This kind of calm and constructive thinking puts you in the right frame of mind to walk this tightrope successfully, and it gives the customer confidence that you are capable of leading them across their tightrope as well.

Be Careful with the Truth

When a professional services consultant is overly frank with a customer, it can easily be perceived as being unprofessional. The manner in which you deliver the naked truth to the customer may very well impact the speed in which the customer accepts it. To make a totally outrageous analogy, imagine telling your friend that his house looked ugly. Overly candid statements of this kind will either put him on the defensive, or he'll dismiss the observation completely. However, if you mention to him that you think the rose bed at the front could do with a little pruning, and then later suggest that the paint is chipping on the front porch, then he is likely to be less defensive and take each observation on its merits.

This isn't to say that you should drip-feed bad news on an engagement, but you do have to remember that the customer will have a sense of pride in what they are trying to accomplish. Hence, you must be diplomatic when identifying to them that there are issues that need resolving and improvements that need to be made. When the truth is delivered too abruptly, it can impair the time it takes for the receiver of that news to really listen to the contents of your statement.

As an example, I often see professional services consultants fall into the blame game, pointing fingers in the hope of immediately trying to realign an expectation. They will say something like, "that is wrong because you guys didn't listen when I told you not to do it." While this statement may be true, it is also confrontational and provocative over a matter that is now largely irrelevant. It no longer matters who did what; what matters now is how we resolve it. Furthermore, a trusted advisor acknowledges human failings with diplomacy, and this type of finger pointing is beneath someone of this status. I often comfort customers or even their individual team members with observations such as "Let's not dwell too long on how we got here. This isn't the first time this has happened on an engagement, and it definitely won't be the last."

When I was younger, I did not fully appreciate the damage the naked truth can have on an engagement. In my early years at IBM, I let myself believe that our sales guys were always overselling us. This kind of misalignment frustrated me to the point of wanting to hit the misaligned expectation with the blunt truth as soon as the engagement started. When meeting with the customer I would say things like, "I'm not sure who told you that, but it can't be done." Wow, what a mistake! This approach forced way too much change on the customer in too short a time and in too abrupt a manner. I was bludgeoning our chances of success to death with the cold hard truth, and I simply needed to learn a better balance.

Over time, I have found that a trusted advisor must care about the customer's suffering, and his or her goal should be to provide aid in their hour of need. This means that difficult news should always be delivered in a direct but empathetic manner. By way of comparison, I once read an article where oncologists were investigating the use of a six-step process for the delivery of bad news to patients that they called S.P.I.K.E.S. While it is not important to detail each letter of this acronym, it is important to note that the intent of the program was to do everything possible to ensure that bad news was delivered directly, but in an empathetic and productive way. The seriousness of the news that oncologists must deliver had them focus on the goals they needed to achieve with their patient. The patient must be in a situation where they are focused and ready to receive the bad news, they must be told directly and unequivocally the seriousness of the situation, but at the same time it was important to maintain hope by immediately putting into place the best strategy possible given the circumstances. While the bad news we are delivering is obviously less serious, a service provider must also have such a tool.

It is also important to be in the right frame of mind when delivering the truth. Yet again, the situation is like a tightrope. A professional services consultant must constantly balance their ability to keep an engagement on realistic footing, while simultaneously avoiding the temptation to be overly-abrupt in doing so. At no time should a professional services consultant mislead a customer, but they should certainly learn the many techniques that will help to soften the blow of bad news. Also, remember that you're working under a contract, and that anything you say or write may be repeated if the two parties should end up in a dispute. Be careful with what you admit to, and focus on resolving the issue, rather than assigning blame. These conversations can be difficult indeed, but in the right frame of mind, the truth can be tactfully delivered in a way that doesn't make the situation worse.

EMPATHY, UNDERSTANDING AND RESOLUTION

Once you have the right frame of mind you can begin the process of realigning the expectation. As we have discussed, these conversations are essential for your engagement to be successful, but they are also full of potential points at which the conversation could escalate further. For this reason, it is crucial that you have a process to follow. I have taught this process to hundreds of people over the years. It gives you a solid framework for walking into a customer meeting and structuring the conversation so that you can maintain control of it. I developed this process one day when sitting with a services professional who was struggling with an angry customer's demands. He was asking if I could jump onto an escalation call because he was uncomfortable with the conversation he had to have with them. I was double booked with another very important meeting so I was trying to convince him that he was capable of handling the situation without me. I explained clearly how I would run the meeting. I told him to structure the conversation in the following way.

1. Demonstrate believable *empathy* to the customer's situation and let them vent without interrupting;

2. Once they have vented, demonstrated a clear **understanding** of the situation from all perspectives;

3. Take ownership of providing a **resolution** to the situation;

The person in question disappeared to make the call and when he returned, he was very excited. The call was very successful, and the approach had worked. This was not his first escalation call with this customer, and this one had gone much better than any of the others. He commented that the process worked to calm the tone of the meeting as well as to provide a clear path forward for both parties. On my way home in my car, I started to dissect the significance of this simple structure.

Empathy

As we have learned, there is a lot at stake for the customer's employees who have internally committed that your services will improve their business. If those improvements are in jeopardy, then the customer's employees are likely to react strongly and sometimes emotionally. This could manifest itself as anger, frustration, disappointment, or even in the form of irrational threats. As an example, I once had a CIO threaten. "I'll ruin you in the valley," referring to my company and the Silicon Valley region. Now that's one hell of a threat.

In situations like this, we often want to jump right in and address the problem immediately, or in the example I just cited, laugh and say "you've got to be kidding." But from the perspective of the upset person, this kind of action can feel as though you're ignoring the significance of their pain and, until you have demonstrated that you truly feel it, you are unlikely to make any headway in getting them back to the table to have a cooperative and constructive discussion.

When having difficult conversations, *let the customer vent.* The reason we call it venting is because it releases the emotional pressure that has built up around the situation. Since discovering the misalignment, the customer may have had to escalate the issue to the executive team and wait for calendars to line up before a face-to-face meeting can be scheduled. During this time, the pressure of the situation continues to increase, as there is no way for it to be relieved until the meeting takes place. Once it does take place, expect fireworks. This release is a perfectly natural reaction to the difficult situation. The customer has been told that the business improvement they have promised others is not going to happen as they expected, which is a very big deal.

Until this pressure is relieved, the people affected are not ready, and in some cases not able, to effectively listen to a resolution, even if it is the right one. During this venting period, you must continue to remain *calm and constructive.* Don't get defensive. Put yourself in their shoes and try to understand how they are feeling-- and validate their feelings as you go. This is empathy.

Empathy is not the same as sympathy. The subtle difference can be confusing, but getting it wrong can profoundly impact the outcome of a difficult conversation. People who are upset with you do not want your sympathy, they want you to understand and acknowledge the level of pain you have caused. A good friend of mine, and editor of this book, explains it as the difference between feeling sorry _for_ someone versus feeling sorry _with_ them. False empathy will come across as cheap sympathy, which can inflame the situation, so it is important that you hone your skill of walking in your customer's shoes and imagine what it must be like to experience this event from their perspective.

Allow the customer to finish their sentences, and only speak when they expect you to speak. Regardless of whether you are at fault, it's never a good idea to cut the customer off mid-sentence to defend yourself. This will only further aggravate the situation, and it is unlikely to clear the air sufficiently to move on to the next step in the process. In order to properly manage the situation, you need to let the customer finish venting, despite how uncomfortable it may make you feel. This is not the time for finger pointing and scapegoating. If the escalation was caused by the customer's own negligence, then you may need to find a solution that aids them in saving face. Assigning blame during this process will only make the customer feel as though you are adding salt to their wounds, and it will do nothing but strain your future relationship.

By the same token, you should also remember that this is not the time for you to admit fault. Given the amount of money that's on the line in a complex engagement, and the possibility that disputes could wind up in court, admitting fault can be very costly to your firm. For this reason, you should learn to empathize without admitting fault. Instead of specifically taking the blame for the existing problem, make general statements that indicate empathy. For example, you can say things like:

"It is not lost upon me how upsetting this situation is for you."

"I too am very disappointed that we find ourselves in this position."

"This is not a situation that we take lightly and you have our full attention."

In order to effectively manage this stage of the discussion, I strongly suggest you take very detailed notes about the customer's stated views. In listening to a customer vent, you must be careful to avoid being misunderstood as implicitly accepting all of the stated viewpoints as correct. For this reason, taking accurate notes will allow you to review precisely what the customer said, and once the venting is finished, you can clarify whether or not you agree with those statements.

Experienced "hot heads" know that if they seem emotional or mad enough when they say something, that people may not challenge their argument. They also know that you may not want to interrupt them for fear of exacerbating their anger. Sometimes, an emotional rant is simply a tactic to prompt everyone to accept the ranting person's viewpoint as the truth. I must confess that as a customer, I too may have been guilty of this once or twice. Experienced consultants know that it is always better to let the customer vent, meanwhile taking copious notes that can be used to correct the facts afterwards under less volatile circumstances. While it is recommend that you always address any objections immediately, you can do so in such a way that you defer their resolution to another time, in the hope of finding a more productive environment for resolution.

The point to remember is that you must stay calm and constructive and not to let other people's emotions sway you away from the principles to which you have committed. Apart from ensuring that you avoid implicitly accepting false statements, you will not regret what you don't say. Saying, agreeing or doing something unprofessional at this stage could be very costly, so adherence to the principles and your own professional demeanor is critical.

There will come a point when the emotion drifts from the conversation, and the focus will switch to the reality of having to deal with the crisis. When your customer has embraced a calm and constructive demeanor, you'll know that this stage is coming to a close and that you've shown empathy effectively. This is when you should shift into the second stage of the process: *understanding*.

Understanding

Now that you and your customer are on the same page as to the seriousness of the situation, it is possible for you to begin resolving it. To do this effectively, you must listen to all of the different viewpoints of the situation and find a way to agree to a common understanding of the issues. This process may require a review of the events that created the problem. During this review, you may once again be tempted to defend yourself. Avoid this temptation here as well. Take care with how you word your statements about these events and avoid attacking your customer's perspective. The primary objective of this step is to gather as many perspectives as possible from the people involved and to unify your understanding of the problem.

Understanding does not mean agreeing. It is okay for issues to remain contentious through this stage, so long as we understand why they are contentious. For example, consider a situation in which the customer believes that the contract's wording gives them full access to your services without additional charge, and you believe this to be incorrect. While the perspectives may conflict, you can both understand it by agreeing that the issue is a difference in opinion about the customer's access to your services. If you don't identify the differing views of the problem in advance then they are likely to surprise you later when you are trying to get consensus on the resolution. This way, you have the more important conversations first, which gives you the complete picture of the issue you are trying to resolve. Demonstrating this depth of character and integrity is something that customers will not forget.

Resolution

Once you've demonstrated empathy and understanding, you're moving in the right direction, but you're not out of the woods yet. Now that everyone is on the same page, you need to take ownership of resolving the problem. Taking ownership means driving the process toward resolving it, even if you're not responsible for the problem itself. If the issue is impeding your ability to provide your customer with a successful engagement, you must take ownership of the process to remove that impediment. This means that you may or may not own some of the actions within the plan to resolve the issue.

If you do not, you should still insist that there be a plan and that you commit to keeping track of its progress. The goal is to ensure that both companies have a clear path to resolve the issue correctly. This is your moment to shine as a trusted advisor, even if you are not going to own any of the resolution. Present your method of resolving the problem like a doctor prescribing treatment for an illness, and work to earn your customer's approval by explaining it properly. If you are to be involved in the resolution, then make sure you set expectations clearly by using *who, what, when and the how(s)* from Principle #3. By taking command of this situation, you will certainly demonstrate your value as a trusted advisor.

Every difficult conversation with a customer should follow the framework of empathy, understanding and resolution. It is the best way to make the most of a difficult situation.

The empathy, understanding, and resolution process allows you to take a seemingly dire situation and create an environment in which you and the customer can overcome it successfully, and at the same time, strengthen your relationship. Between my teams, and myself we have probably employed this method thousands of times. Everyone who adopts it swears that it is the best approach to handling these situations. To some degree, it even takes some of the fear out of having these conversations because you have the comfort of a proven process to fall back on. Get used to using this method, and you will begin to see that each difficult conversation is an opportunity to progress further towards success. Become familiar with structuring your difficult conversations this way, and you'll surely make the best of what feels like a bad situation.

SELLING THE RESOLUTION

Just like your sales team had to give your a customer a sales *pitch* to convince them to buy your services, you too need to do the same when asking your customer to adopt your recommended resolution. There may be multiple ways to resolve the misaligned expectation, and you and the customer may differ in your opinion as to how to do that. To pitch your solution successfully, you should deploy techniques similar to those of a sales pitch. Obviously, you should always remain calm and constructive, but you may also need to deploy one or several of the following techniques.

Focus on the Outcome

As we have discussed, the customer is after an outcome, so remain focused on that. Sometimes people will argue profusely about the process to resolve an issue, rather than simply focusing on whether or not that process will substantially impact the quality and success of the final result. It can sometimes be beneficial to bring this fact up during the conversation. "Do we really need to argue about the process we are going to use when the result is going to be the same?"

Be Prescriptive

While focusing on the outcome, you should also be able to use your influence as a trusted advisor to prescribe how the customer can achieve their desired outcome. I spoke about *Prescribing Done* in "Principle #2: Always Know What *Done* Looks Like," and that technique is critically important when getting a customer to accept your proposed solution. The technique requires you to use your expert status to strongly recommend a path to success. Going against the recommendation of the expert is a tough decision for the customer to make.

Yes, if...

If the customer proposes an alternative, you should respond respectfully. If you prefer your own solution, you should tactfully steer the customer back to your method. Be aware of the negativity the word "no" carries as it can make you seem close-minded. Instead, consider redirecting customers with "Yes, if..." This approach can be used without making you appear negative. For example, perhaps you recommend that the customer's team complete a specific action to resolve an issue. The customer then counters your proposal and asks that you do the work instead. You can push the customer back to your original proposal by saying, "Yes we could do that, if we are willing to expand the project's budget to account for that work."

Here, you have responded positively, but also indicated the customer's budget will need to increase. It is preferable that a customer sees the consequence of their own recommendation and declines to accept it rather than have you shoot it down without consideration. This may seem minor, and you may ultimately need to say "no" to a bad suggestion if the customer persists, but using "yes, if..." permits you to defend your proposed resolutions while retaining your image as a calm and constructive service provider.

REALLY DIFFICULT CONVERSATIONS

From this point forward, this chapter deals with disaster scenarios: i.e. situations where all of the standard, success-oriented tactics have failed, and you and the customer cannot agree on how to realign the expectations. In such cases, the situation will likely escalate to an experienced engagement manager, or even a professional services executive, and now some *really* difficult conversations need to take place. These situations are rare, but when they occur, it is likely that the most experienced people within your firm should be dealing with them.

Leverage Failure

The first and most viable option is to leverage failure. This means leveraging the fact that neither party wants the engagement to fail, nor for it to end up in a costly legal dispute. Such failures are a huge distraction to the customer, and you will find that in most cases the customer is more willing to settle for something close to their expectation rather than accept failure. Hence, your senior executives may direct your project team to discontinue services on an engagement until the issue is resolved. While this is a harsh action to take, it draws attention to the need for an equitable resolution, and it typically works very well.

I once worked for a company where we successfully took this approach on a portfolio of 70 separate customer engagements, amongst which 40 were already losing money. Because they were contracted at various fixed prices, we were hemorrhaging money on these engagements, and each of them had already cost us more than the price we had agreed with the customer. These engagements were generating no revenue so we were losing 100% of the cost to have someone work them. The financial losses on these engagements were uncapped; there was no limit to how much we could lose on each engagement, so we had to stop them from bleeding our profits dry. In each situation, we had a binding contract that clearly made us accountable to provide an outcome for the price agreed. We were so backed into a corner, however, that we had to fight our way out. We did this by walking in to each engagement and saying, "We are no longer going to be able to work on this engagement unless we can find a way to get paid for the services we are providing."

The theory behind this strategy is that customers don't want to end up in legal dispute and would rather lose ground and begin paying for some of the services they are receiving rather than have the engagement die and go down the path of litigation. About 12 months after starting this strategy, we resolved all 40 engagements without even the threat of a lawsuit. About 90% of the engagements changed so that the customer started paying for at least some of our time, and the rest were either killed by the customer or the customer paid someone else to finish the job for them. Fortunately, none of them ever decided that legal action was a productive use of their time because the truth is that it rarely benefits either party. Each customer knew that they were taking advantage of my company's poor decision to provide them such a contract in the first place. Very few of them were surprised about our decision to draw a harder line. We didn't want to be rude or disrespectful; we just couldn't survive as a company if these contracts weren't halted immediately.

My point is that that even in difficult and heated moments, nobody really wants your engagement to fail. Don't mistake this as a sign that customers won't just shut engagements down and kill them if they become too difficult or the engagement's ROI begins to look doubtful. They do this all the time so you need to avoid over-leveraging failure, but on the whole, most customers would rather finish an engagement and get slightly less than what they were expecting than to explain to their executive stakeholders that it failed entirely.

Unfortunately, Sometimes You Have to Put a Bullet in it

As I just described, in rare and extreme circumstances, it simply becomes necessary to put the proverbial bullet in the engagement and walk away from it. After you've tried to leverage failure, your company may determine that the only option left is be "done," rather than being "successful." As you're probably aware, the phrase "put a bullet in it" refers to the action a farmer takes once he has decided that the cost of keeping a farm animal alive is too high in comparison with the future value it could provide. Deciding whether an animal has outlived its usefulness is painful, and it is never be taken lightly, but sometimes it must be done. This decision is similarly painful for the service provider's executives when the time arrives to consider it as an option.

In an engagement where failure looms large and *leveraging failure* did not get the engagement back on track, then the service provider must evaluate whether it is simply too much of a liability to continue. If getting the engagement back on track seems too difficult or too costly, then it may be time to put it out of its misery and face whatever consequences may follow. This requires a thorough cost-benefit analysis. Will the cost of killing the engagement save enough money to compensate for the losses that may be incurred if you continue to try to complete it?

We can often feel so close to finishing an engagement that we convince ourselves that just one more week will get us over the line. There is a point however, at which this hope become futile. Once we realize that a successful outcome is not going to be achieved without incurring unbearable costs, we must turn our focus to being *done* instead of successful. There is no precise formula to arrive at this conclusion, and, in fact, many companies evaluate this in differing and subjective ways. Different companies put varying values on the loss of a customer depending on many different tangible and intangible calculations.

Clearly, decisions like this belong to senior management, but this book intends to provide you with a complete view of the world of professional services, and this is the harsh reality. Not all engagements succeed, and you should understand the role you play in making an engagement a success rather than a failure. Having difficult conversations early is the most valuable principle in this respect.

Nobody wants to work on a failed engagement. While failure can be hard to swallow, it does happen. Putting a bullet in a failing engagement represents a way to deliberately fall off the professional services tightrope and land somewhere safe with only minor injuries. When done correctly, this decision prevents you from walking further out over the canyon only to fall farther and suffer much greater consequences.

FIELD EXAMPLE: TYING IT ALL TOGETHER

To help illustrate how difficult situations play out in real life, I am going to describe a situation I recently encountered. While it is somewhat lengthy, it will provide you with a situation that at first glance seems difficult to resolve. However, by applying the concepts of this chapter, I will illustrate how we stepped through a process of quickly resolving it. In doing so, you will gain an appreciation for how to apply these concepts yourself.

The Situation

I had just joined a young software company that had a small services team that was completely overwhelmed. The team of about eight services consultants was working on 80 different engagements that were all "in progress." The delivery model we had adopted was that of a hands-off approach wherein we provided some design assistance, but the customer or another professional services firm provided the implementation services. The team was completely distressed, their customers were unhappy, and they needed help. Upon my initial investigation into the situation, here is what I discovered:

- The software was sold under a Software-As-A-Service model. This meant that the customer had purchased the first twelve months of access to the software. After that period, the customer would decide if the software was providing value and would either renew for another twelve months or decide to stop paying all together.

- While there was debate over the value of the hands-off approach, there were some contributing and unchangeable factors that made it impossible to change this model in the short term.

- In well over 75% of the eighty engagements, the customer had already had the software for more than four months. This meant that over a third of the first year's subscription had passed. The time for us to demonstrate value for these customers was diminishing fast. If we could not get the customer live and provide them with value soon, there was no way that they would consider paying for another year at full price.

- In almost 30% of the eighty engagements, the customer was inactive and still looking for a development team to implement the software we had sold them. When I joined this company, we seemed to consider this issue the customer's problem. The reality, however, was that an inactive customer was almost certain to cancel their contract upon its first renewal.

- In a different 50% of the eighty engagements, we seemed to be unable to identify the customer's executive stakeholder.

- A good number of customers were asking for different enhancements in order for the software to satisfy their expectations. The customers were saying that they could not go live until our software could do what they wanted.

- The eight resources on my team were also serving as pre-sales support and assisting the customer support team in answering support tickets from customers who were already live. The professional services team was not able to focus on their core responsibility of getting customers live.

Before we continue, you should review this list carefully and identify which issues you would consider the most important. To some degree, they all have a level of importance but in resolving the situation, some are far less important than others.

What Was Important?

The first issue we tackled was the continual diversion to urgent assistance of other departments. By responding to these *urgent* requests for help, we were not leaving ourselves enough time to focus on the *important* task of getting customers live.

While the actions of the professional services team were well intentioned, the diversion to the urgent matters was masking the real problem. The real issue was that the other departments were undermanned and their constant requests for assistance were delaying our ability to service our projects. Once this was identified, it was a much easier problem to fix. Of course, we continued to support the other departments as we made the transition, but thankfully, we were now addressing the real and important issue.

With this decision, we began to get some of our time back as the other departments hired in new resources. This still left us with the important challenge of getting our engagements back on track. After careful consideration, we determined that the most important issue to resolve was that of us not having executive stakeholders on the engagements. As we have discussed previously, the customer's executive stakeholder is the one who cares most about the engagement's success or failure, and they are the person who vouched for the value of the engagement's outcome. If nobody within the customer's team had anything riding on success or failure of the engagement, then nobody of importance cared about its outcome. It didn't matter what other issues needed resolving, these engagements were unlikely to ever to be successful until someone of importance was going to make it a priority to resolve them.

The Difficult Conversations

We decided that if a customer could not assign an executive stakeholder, then were going to stop working their engagement. Customers who really cared about achieving an outcome with our software reacted swiftly and assigned an executive stakeholder. For those that didn't, we stopped working their engagements entirely.

While you may think this is a harsh response, the reality is that those customers without executive stakeholders were already unlikely to renew their agreements with us. There was simply nobody in the customer's organization who cared enough about the engagement to resolve the other issues (such as finding the resources to do the implementation). All we did was accelerate our understanding of which customers still wanted to make use of the software, and which customers had already decided that the benefits that had been promised were no longer worth pursuing. There was nothing stopping a customer from coming back to us when they had identified an executive stakeholder (which some did).

Most importantly, this stopped us chasing failure and wasting our time. This added bandwidth increased our ability to serve the customers who really wanted to progress their engagements forward. Combined with the time we had recouped from not chasing urgent requests from other departments, we were able to whittle our list of in-progress projects down to 40 within four months. Because we were no longer slowed down by the burden of dying engagements, we were able to get new customers live much faster, which made them much happier with our software and our company.

What Was Unimportant?

While there is no single *least* important issue in the list above, let's discuss one issue that was unimportant enough for us to ignore. I have often found that this issue exists frequently in professional services firms that live inside of larger product companies. It is the issue of the customer wanting the product to have new capabilities before they will use it. While this can be an important request, product change is outside of the professional services team's control. Additively, it takes a long time to make such changes and the customer was sure to stop paying for the software until those changes were made. Hence, the issue is important and potentially urgent for the product development or engineering department in charge of building the products, but it is far less important for the professional services team.

However, it *is* important for the professional services team to focus the customer on finding value from the software as it exists *today*. Tomorrow's version of the software is never guaranteed to eventuate, so delaying the engagement until those capabilities are delivered is a huge gamble to take. You are betting that your customer will wait around long enough for those improvements to eventuate before losing interest in what you had originally promised them. Once a customer stops working actively on an engagement, their team will be assigned to other important activities and the desire to achieve an outcome from your services disappears. Reacquiring enough momentum from the company's decision makers to once again fund and sponsor the engagement may be very difficult or even impossible. In the field of sales, they say "time kills all deals," and, in a professional services environment, it also kills all engagements!

The more productive approach in this situation is to focus on the outcomes that are within the professional services team's control. If you can convince the customer that there is still value to be extracted from today's version of the product, then you should continue with the engagement. This ensures that the customer receives some immediate benefit, and it also buys you more time to make the necessary product changes for them in the future.

What This Field Example Illustrates

This example illustrates a number of situations you may face on an engagement. The first is the line between urgent and important is not always clear, and it can change dramatically between divisions within the same firm. It would have been irresponsible for me to stop servicing urgent requests from other departments, but it was more important that I assisted them in building that capability.

The second situation you are likely to face is that sometimes there is no avoiding the inevitable cost that an engagement is likely to suffer. In the above situation, there was no magic wand to somehow recover the situation and make everyone happy. There is a fine line between being optimistic and giving it your all and blindly trying to achieve success in the face of imminent failure. The ability to accurately predict an engagement's success or disaster comes with experience. However, if you understand this book's principles, then you should be able to identify the signs you are looking for.

In my field example, the cost of supporting the dying engagements was robbing our time from those that truly wanted to thrive. By channeling our efforts into the right engagements, we had determined which engagements would cost us, how much they would cost us and when it would happen. Once we had accepted our fate, the degree to which it was going to affect us was in our hands. To continue to serve all of our engagements poorly would have resulted in a higher rate of failure and uncontrollable costs. As we discussed earlier, success is always our primary objective, but in some cases we will just need to settle for *done*! The sooner we are able to understand which one we are aiming for, the more successful we will be.

The final point is that you have to look at the big picture and decide which issues deserve difficult conversations. There is no point having a difficult conversation about an issue that is not going to bring about significant results. In the heat of an engagement with lots of urgent issues flying about, it is easy to become hell-bent on having a difficult conversation about something that is urgent but not important and hence resolving it. Unfortunately, doing so brings little real benefit to the engagement's chances of success. Difficult conversations are hard enough without forcing yourself to have more of them than you need.

CHAPTER SUMMARY

Walking the professional services tightrope is not for the faint of heart. An engagement can present many dangerous situations to the professional services consultant, and you must be ready to handle them correctly. You must be able to identify them and take the right corrective action to ensure the safety of yourself, your team, and your customer. Ignoring the dangers doesn't make them go away. It only keeps them alive and provides them a greater opportunity of causing you more damage in the future.

This business requires difficult conversations constantly. Things will go wrong. People will make mistakes. Expectations will become misaligned. Resolving these misalignments demands you demonstrate career-defining integrity and strength of character. If done correctly, you will be known for putting the customer's needs first, which will inspire the customer's trust in your recommendations. While difficult conversations can be unpleasant, they also present you with a unique opportunity to shine. Manage them properly, and you will prosper; avoid them, and you may never recover.

THINK F.A.A.S.T.

"Excellence is an art won by training and habituation. We do not act rightly because we have virtue or excellence, but we rather have those because we have acted rightly. We are what we repeatedly do. Excellence, then, is not an act but a habit"

– Aristotle

KEEP CALM AND CARRY ON

For the ill prepared, a crisis can trigger the desire to react with an unplanned action, or worse, to be paralyzed by fear and to not react at all. On a high wire, a situation such as a sudden change in wind direction, or a momentary twitch of the wire could trigger such a reaction. A tightrope walker must not overreact to such events despite the immense amount of risk they are undertaking. Instead, they must stop, and focus their attention on the fundamentals of regaining balance before moving one. This ability to fall back onto a learned habit is taught by many professions as way to increase the chance of success in the most trying of times. Hence, I think it is invaluable that we, in the professional services industry, have a similar tool in our kit bag.

Many armed forces units face a similar challenge in that well-trained cadets can still freeze or panic during a gunfight. For this reason, they train men and women who carry arms to react calmly and constructively in such a situation by reciting a mnemonic known as B.R.A.S.S. This is an acronym that stands for

Breathe, Relax, Aim, Sight and Squeeze, and it is an easy-to-remember process for firing a weapon accurately. By having recruits use this process under simulated battle conditions, it becomes ingrained as their default reaction in such a circumstance. It becomes a forced, but potentially life-saving, habit.

The habit that a professional services consultant must exhibit in a time of crisis is to *deliver a quality service*. Regardless of how bad, or how dire a situation seems, the customer is paying for the expert to act as a trusted advisor. Such an advisor does not panic or freeze in the face of failure. He or she is expected (and paid) to focus on the customer's success and find a way to succeed.

TURNING QUALITY INTO A HABIT

To *"deliver a quality service"* is a very subjective statement. Different customers will measure the same service in different ways. While there are likely to be similarities in their observations, independent ratings of the same service will vary. This is because individuals define a *quality service* based upon their differing experiences.

Likewise, if you were to ask five of your peers to define a quality service they would each tell you similar but varying definitions of it. The differences between their answers would highlight why services teams find it so hard to deliver quality consistently. Without a consistent definition of quality, the individuals within a team are all working towards a different level of it, which also means that they are all working to a slightly different version of what *done* should look like.

While the principles you have read thus far all define a level of quality that every professional services consultant must exhibit, there is still a need for a principle that can be called upon in a time of crisis. Such a principle could act as the learned habit that kicks in when a professional services consultant's balance is threatened. I have spent a lot of time trying to develop a perspective on how to teach such a habit. I have found that it is too easy to fall into the trap of flooding individuals with engagement metrics like customer satisfaction and budget accuracy as a way to measure their service quality. Such metrics are nothing but measurements of past results. They look backward at an outcome that cannot be altered. While there is value in learning from past outcomes, it offers little guidance to the consultant on how to act when a different crisis occurs. To have any chance of making quality a habit we require a forward-looking principle that provides a way to rebalance at the first sign of falling from the tightrope.

Turning this principle into a habit has a far-reaching effect because it helps cease the seemingly endless firefighting that occurs in out-of-control professional services teams. Such a situation creates a stream of urgent distractions that are unimportant to the higher priority of fixing the root causes of the escalations. This means that every new escalation just robs another engagement of the time required to keep it on the path to success. Hence, the professional services team starts to run back and forth reacting to escalations instead of spending the time required to avoid them. This tires a team of consultants quickly and it can cause burn out in those who are hardworking and dedicated. Such a loss of top and dedicated talent in this situation only further serves to exacerbate it.

Thankfully, you *can* get this situation under control. Over the years, I have worked with my management teams to create and refine a framework for communicating service quality. In doing so I have seen teams change behavior in significant ways in a very short period of time. By adopting it across an entire team, it has the potential to instill a learned habit that can be called upon uniformly in a time of crisis.

THINKING F.A.A.S.T.

From the perspective of a professional services consultant, a quality service consists of five core traits that must be exhibited throughout an engagement. Each trait is easily identifiable and, when considered in the context of a given situation, can provide guidance on how to act. It gives the professional services consultant a *cheat sheet* that can be called upon at any time to help identify the right way to handle an unexpected situation. This is an incredibly useful tool, which I have employed in the form of an acronym that I term F.A.A.S.T.

Focus

Attention to Detail

Accountable

Skilled

Trustworthy

Each of these five attributes describe a specific trait or characteristic that we expect of a professional services consultant. A consultant who fails to exhibit any one of these is not going to achieve success repeatedly. Each characteristic is vital to delivering a quality service, and each member of the team must employ and exhibit them at all times throughout the engagement. If you think back to almost any mistake or avoidable situation you've suffered during an engagement, I'm fairly confident you can review this list and identify which traits you overlooked. For a professional services consultant to achieve success, you must demand these five characteristics from yourself so that they become a part of your instinctive behavior on every customer engagement.

At some point, you may inadvertently neglect one of these characteristics, but you should also expect to be able to regain your focus on it at will. Each attribute is actionable and identifies the behavior that you should exhibit. The more you can combine these traits to react to situations and employ them in your day to-day activities, the better your professional services performance will be.

F.A.A.S.T. is an acronym that makes it easy to recall the important elements required to save the situation, even in high-pressure situations. The word from which the acronym is derived (*fast*) is an ironic reminder that in such moments you should actually slow down. Although you should embrace the attributes of F.A.A.S.T., you should not do so in too fast a manner. In times of distress, we have talked about the value of being *calm and constructive*. In creating the acronym, I found the irony worked well in serving as a reminder that sometimes we have to go slow to *Think F.A.A.S.T.*

FOCUS

As a professional services consultant, you must always be focused on your customer's outcomes. The customer is paying for your time, and they expect that you will be attentive to all matters regarding their success. Despite your efforts, it can be very easy for a professional services consultant to lose focus. Maybe you are working on too many engagements. Maybe you have other things going on in your life that are commanding your attention, or maybe you are stuck in the minutiae and the detail is distracting you from the big picture. In these situations, you can regain your focus by simply considering the following questions:

- Am I focused on the same outcome the customer is focused on?

- What is my role in achieving that outcome?

- Am I focused on achieving progress towards that outcome today?

- Is my focus aligned with agreed version of *Done*

If you answered "No," or "I Don't Know," to any of these questions above, then you need to reconsider your focus. You are unlikely to remember all of these questions verbatim, but simply learning them (and remembering to assess your focus) will give you the necessary guidance. Without being focused on the right elements of your engagement, a successful outcome is unlikely.

You should also apply this trait of *focus* to your career. Are you focused on the right things to ensure success within your current job role? You can evaluate your focus by asking yourself the following questions:

- Am I focused on the next step in my career plan?

- Am I focused on my team and how I can best help those around me?

Again, a "No" or "I Don't Know" to either of these questions requires an adjustment to your focus.

ATTENTION TO DETAIL

This book has frequently addressed the dangers of getting too bogged down in the detail. While this is true, I must emphasize that the problem lies in getting *bogged down* and not in the *detail*. Attention to detail is a critical element of quality because it represents the precise level of execution the customer expects from you. Your ability to master the customer's complex details will always be a critical component in delivering a quality service.

A service provider's ability to become appropriately immersed in the details of the customer's business is crucial to providing their desired outcomes. In our haste to complete the engagement on time, we must remember that our endeavor to discover and absorb the customer's detail must also be done accurately. Inaccurate detail collection creates expectation gaps, and we know where those will lead. On the contrary, if we take too much time to collect details, or we collect more detail than we need, then we are wasting precious engagement time. Hence, to dive into the appropriate depth of their details, we employ a process called *functional decomposition*.

Although this term sounds complex, it simply means that a service provider should draw a box around each area of a customer's problems and then break each box down into its components parts in such a way that the sub-components still add up to the whole. This ensures that we don't miss important details. If the sum of the components does not equal the whole, we are missing something. This approach permits you to collect detail about a subject while ensuring that you don't get lost in it.

This technique is often employed as a way to break down a larger problem into smaller and more manageable components. When using this technique for something like a project plan, the service provider begins by describing *done* as merely one deliverable, which is the customer's desired outcome. An example of this would be something like "The Finished Product." The service provider then breaks down that particular deliverable into its sub-deliverables. This process is repeated for each deliverable and results in a hierarchy of deliverables that will combine to form the entirety of the customer's desired outcome.

For project planning specifically, this hierarchy is called a Work Breakdown Structure (WBS) but the process used to build one (functional decomposition) is as a general tool that can be employed in other areas such as problem solving. To apply it as problem solving tool, you simply treat the problem as a final deliverable and continue to break it down into its sub-deliverables so that they are easier to inspect. You continue to do this until you have found the deliverable that isn't working correctly. Ensuring that the parts always add up to the whole helps make sure that you don't overlook anything.

When do you stop breaking down a component? Even after some research, it is clear that there is no precise rule to this question, only a number of "rules of thumb." Personally, I was taught to stop breaking a WBS down once I could easily and accurately estimate the effort required to build that deliverable. We called this an "autonomous work package." While I have found it hard to find a reference to this term, I believe it means that the work package itself is self-explanatory to the point of not needing any further explanation. In other words it reaches the point where breaking it down further serves no purpose. This same principle should be applied when you are diving into the details of your customer's business. Until you have obtained everything you need to forge a path to your customer's success, you should continue to dive into those details. Once you can ascertain that further detail will not benefit your cause, you must stop.

Attention to detail is yet another tightrope you must walk. Ignore the details and they will hurt your engagement, but dive too far into them and you'll be distracted from what is truly important. This means you must surface from the depths of your detailed discovery every now and then and ensure that you are still heading in the right direction. You cannot waste time gathering details that are irrelevant to achieving a successful outcome. Without focusing your attention on the right level of detail, you cannot provide a quality service.

ACCOUNTABLE

We often use the word *accountable* to describe our strengths to others, but this description of ourselves may fail to incorporate the degree of accountability required of a professional services consultant. In our professional sphere, there are four somewhat symbiotic systems of accountability in operation, all of which must function simultaneously and remain accountable to each other. These four systems function together to make the delivery of a quality service possible. No individual system can fail without severely impacting the other three in a way that makes success highly doubtful. To truly deliver a quality service, the following four systems of accountability must be in place simultaneously.

Accountability to Your Own Firm

As an individual professional services provider, you must be accountable to your firm. Your firm sends you out into the field each day with its valuable information. If you are not accountable to them, success is almost impossible. Your accountability to your firm requires that you:

- be skilled in the area in which you are performing your duties;

- know the goals of your firm and team;

- know the goals of the engagements you are working on;

- own the quality to which you execute your tasks;

- communicate and collaborate with your team members as necessary;

- contribute to your company's collective best practices (referred to later as the Collective Wisdom);

- look for opportunities where your skills can help the firm grow;

Your Firm's Accountability to You

Your employer must reciprocate your accountability by providing the same to you. An employer cannot expect accountability from its employees if the employer is not accountable to provide a safe and productive work environment. In return for your accountability, your employer is also accountable to provide you with:

- an environment conducive to honest discussion and feedback;

- the opportunity for each employee to fulfill his or her assigned duties;

- objective and fair feedback to all employees;

- clear company and team goals;

- recognition for positive behavior and results;

- constructive feedback and corrective guidance for areas of improvement;

- access to materials that describe the goals of each engagement;

- fair and objective access to ongoing training budgets if available;

- fair and objective assessment of individuals for promotion;

You and Your Team's Accountability to Your Customer

You cannot deliver customer success until you openly accept that you are accountable to do so. Accountability in this area will help individuals build a successful career, and it will help teams deliver customer success repeatedly. As a service provider you must be accountable to:

- ensure that your engagement's success is the primary driver for all decisions;

- provide constructive guidance and feedback when you think the customer is making a bad or ill-informed decision;

- act quickly and resolve issues as soon as possible to prevent unnecessary costs;

- attempt to complete the engagement on-time and on-budget;

- communicate progress clearly and provide realistic estimates of the effort required to complete your assigned tasks;

Your Customer's Accountability to You and Your Firm

As we discussed in the chapter *Always Know What Done Looks Like*, you must hold the customer accountable for certain essential items required for success on your engagement. Without your customer being accountable for these items, your engagement will undoubtedly be a struggle. As a reminder, here they are again. You must hold your customer accountable to:

- provide you with access to the necessary people and resources required for you to complete your engagement on time;

- act with urgency to provide feedback and make necessary decisions in a timely manner;

- ensure that their staff remains courteous and professional;

- provide a safe work environment for your staff;

- agree and sign off on specifications when required;

- pay for your services in accordance with the terms of the contract;

SKILLED

In the previous section, I mentioned that you must be accountable by exhibiting proficiency in the duties you perform. However, there is an element of proficiency that is specific to delivering a quality service. That element is that you are *always deploying your skills for the customer's benefit.*

Every engagement is an opportunity for you to demonstrate your skills. Customers want your help, so remember that it is important that you bring all of your skills to the engagement every day. It is also important to remember that customers don't want to be distracted by unconstructive skills, so it is equally important to keep your desire to impress them in balance.

You must also be passionate about increasing your own skill levels. Elite athletes work tirelessly at improving the basic skills of their chosen sport, and it is their ability to hone those basics beyond the ordinary that makes them elite. The skills you possess are no different than those of an elite athlete. They should be continuously honed and practiced. Are you junior grade or are you elite grade? You should observe the people around you and constantly analyze which of your colleagues has honed their skills beyond the ordinary and begin to determine how to emulate them so that you too can achieve the same level of mastery.

Remember the premise of this book: successful professional services delivery requires more than just great technical skills. You could be the greatest person in the world at deploying the skills of a project manager, but if you don't round it out with the principles contained in these pages, then your success is doubtful. You often hear people talk about the "soft skills." These are traditionally skills such as presenting, writing, negotiating, and tact.

Don't underestimate the value of soft skills to the progress of your professional services career. The principles provided within this book will turn these soft skills into tools that you can employ to further enhance the technical skills you already have. The more you refine them, the more powerful they become. When your success is riding on how well you help others achieve their goals, your soft skills are what differentiate you from the ordinary.

TRUSTWORTHY

We have talked a lot about trust throughout this book, so it is no surprise to see it appear in an acronym defining the characteristics of professional services quality. It could be argued that being focused, attentive to detail, accountable, and skilled will earn you the customer's trust. The fact however, is that failing to be *trustworthy* could easily undo all of it! It is little things that a service provider may consider innocuous that may be deemed as offensive by the customer that can mar an otherwise successful engagement. There are numerous areas of an engagement that leave room to create distrust between the customer and an individual professional services consultant, some of which we haven't yet examined in this book.

You have promised to make your customer's success a priority, and they will watch you closely to make sure that you do. If you act in a manner that prompts them to perceive otherwise, you may unwittingly breach their trust in a manner that will adversely affect their perception of you and your team. Although the following list is not exhaustive, it will give you an idea of how ordinary actions may be misinterpreted in such a way that they damage the trust you are trying to earn.

- Rounding up timecard hours;

- Over-billing hours (even if accidental);

- Requesting additional payment for every little change, while sometimes necessary to balance budgets, it can make the customer feels as though they are being *nickeled and dimed*;

- Not giving the customer an update on the project financials until the project budget is almost gone;

- Consistently turning up late to the customer's office (even if you are going to work at your firm's office first);

- Leaving early too often;

- Not being present for difficult conversations that concern your area of expertise or control;

- Repeatedly providing late deliverables, or providing them late without taking the lateness of the delivery seriously;

- Being consistently late to or missing meetings;

- Being overly sociable or not being sociable enough;

- Volunteering too much private information;

- Being abrasive in your communication;

- Not standing your ground in difficult circumstances;

- Not being firm enough in your recommendations;

Deep in our fifth principle, we find yet another delicate tightrope to walk. I have instructed you to push customers, hold them accountable, prescribe their success when it's necessary, and force them into difficult conversations. All of this is difficult enough to do with people you know, let alone with your customer who you do not know as well. Furthermore, I've instructed that while you do these things, you must also earn their trust as an individual, and hopefully get them to like you personally! Obviously, this is a very difficult balance. You must be part diplomat, part authoritarian, and part humanitarian. When a person can do all of these while still creating the perception they are affable, they are said to be an *iron fist in a velvet glove*. He or she is capable of being the strong-willed force for good, but in ever such a lovely way.

Over time, you will learn how to find the appropriate balance required to exhibit these traits and earn your customer's trust. Practice is the key. Be charismatic, but not egotistical. Be firm, but fair. Be polite, but in some instances immovable. It would be difficult enough to strike the right balance among these traits in a non-judgmental social setting, let alone in the pressure of a critical work environment. And yet, if you watch how others do it around you, and if you witness how they strike a balance, you will likely be able to do this yourself. Observing others will allow you to determine how you may be able to strike that same balance using the charisma and personality you already have. If you force it, it is likely to look that way and, before you know it, the customer will think you are a phony, and they'll cease to believe you have integrity.

My greatest piece of advice on this matter is to be yourself. Absorb these traits into the personality you already have and be as natural as possible.

If you simply trust yourself and be who you are, I sincerely believe that in the long run, you'll find that people will trust you. From time to time, I see people try to fake their way through this, but it never works for very long. Maybe they pull it off for a few months or even a year, but the truth is that in the business of person-to-person service delivery, your true colors will eventually shine through. Even if your true colors have rough edges or you're outwardly abrasive, you are not precluded from success. You can always soften rough edges, and even abrasive people can be a force for good! Simply put, provided you're willing to accept your personal flaws and work at refining them, you can always find a way to counterbalance your negatives.

FIELD EXAMPLE: CRISIS MODE

Now that we have defined how you can think F.A.A.S.T., lets illustrate how it can be applied to a real world situation. A good friend of mine, and a one-time member of my management team, John Pora is an experienced professional services executive. John has worked with some of the largest customers in the world in delivering complex engagements in high-pressure environments.

I have asked John to recount a time when he found himself in a situation that required more than just the usual engagement delivery principles. As you will see, the concepts of the previous four principles are still applied in this example, but the precision required of the team's execution and the price to be paid for failure are ratcheted to the point of needing something extra. That something "extra" is thinking F.A.A.S.T.

"It was Saturday night and my phone rang out from the living room. I was sure that it was my team calling to provide the status of an upgrade project that we were implementing over the weekend. This was the upgrade of a mission critical and complex phone system for a large financial institution. The upgrade had started after the close of business on Friday and had to be completed by the opening bell on Monday. To my surprise, it was actually our customer calling to advise me that they believed our upgrade was now at risk of failing. They were having grave concerns that the upgrade was not going to be done on time, which would surely have meant a financial loss for them come Monday morning.

I called the project manager for the engagement immediately. Upon inquiry, I discovered that nothing had gone right for my team. The original hardware and software that had been delivered to be used in the upgrade was failing. They tried desperately to get this software up and running but to no avail. They had just failed yet another attempt to upgrade the system with an entirely new set of equipment that had been ordered in at short notice. I could tell that the project manager and his team were sleep deprived and not making good decisions. With only 30 hours or so before the opening bell, it was crisis mode. I had to step into the projects, take control, and think F.A.A.S.T.

Our **focus** was wrong and it needed to be corrected. At this late stage, there was no point trying to achieve success. It was time to put the customer's needs first and make the decision to rollback to the original hardware and software. An inoperable phone system on Monday morning would cost the customer millions in lost revenue. A working phone system was better than no system at all. I had to re-focus my team on ensuring that we had adequate time to uninstall all of the new equipment and reinstall the old stuff. While this was disappointing for everyone, it was at a point where we had to accept failure. Additionally, I needed a new team. My current team was so exhausted that they could not focus. Their poor decision-making had led us down a path of chasing our tails almost to the point of disaster and it was time to send them home for some rest. This newfound focus gave us a fighting chance of saving the situation for the customer.

The decision to rollback to the old system was easy enough, but we were running out of time fast. We needed to work at twice normal speed just to restore the old phone system in time. Rather than allow my team to become frantic and create the kind of thrashing that takes two steps forward, only to be forced one step back; I took the time to focus our **_attention on the details_**. We developed a detailed rollback plan that was far more specific than any plan I have seen for such an endeavor. We could not afford for anything to go wrong. I was banking that our attention to detail would help save the day by having us incur fewer errors along the way, and it did.

While I took personal **_accountability_**, I ensured that our firm as a whole illustrated our commitment to the customer. My team had let us down by not being accountable as trusted advisors and we needed to do everything we could to repair that damage. I explained the situation to our SVP of Engineering and our CEO and they both called the customer and became involved in the situation. This demonstrated that I was accountable to my executives to fix the situation, as well as the fact that our company was now committed to resolving this issue at the highest possible level.

Swapping out the teams allowed me to hand pick the people I needed. We needed a team **_skilled_** specifically in delivering a rollback of this size and complexity. While the original team would have eventually completed the job, I needed the "SWAT Team" to achieve something amazing.

After engaging my CEO and SVP of Engineering we decided that the fees for rolling back the system would not be charged to the customer. We were attempting to demonstrate that we were **_trustworthy_** enough to make the tough decisions when needed and accept the part we played in the situation. We had damaged our relationship with the customer, so it was critical that we cease doing *any further damage and begin repairing it. We should have pulled the pin on the upgrade on Saturday morning and ensured enough time to rollback, but instead, we were scrambling. We explained that we understood our failings immediately and prescribed a solution to regain a workable solution for Monday. While this was not meeting with the original objective, it was definitely making the best of a bad situation.*

Ultimately, we rolled the customer back to their original phone system. That next week we spent a lot of time with our engineering team analyzing what went wrong and reapplying many of the F.A.A.S.T. concepts. We identified the root cause of our issues and discovered that we needed a different combination of hardware and software than we had expected. The following weekend we upgraded the customer and moved them onto the new system. The customer was very pleased that we had saved the day, but this of course made them very weary of purchasing future upgrades from us. We had to work really hard to regain their trust. This included continuing to do some other work for less money than we would normally have agreed. Making the situation right cost us a lot of money, but we retained a very valuable customer, which in the long run served our business well."

Thinking F.A.A.S.T. is a learned habit that can guide you out of the most difficult of circumstances and lead you towards the quality service you wish to provide.

CHAPTER SUMMARY

Just as a tightrope walker must fall back on a solid foundation of basic instincts to overcome an unexpected situation, you too need a foundation that helps you to deliver quality in dangerous customer situations. The principle of *Thinking F.A.A.S.T.* provides you with a framework to employ in times when you need something more than the other principles to overcome a crisis. Remember that the principles incorporated in the acronym F.A.A.S.T. reminds you that service quality consists of being focused, attentive to detail, accountable, skilled and trustworthy. Exhibit these traits in front of the customer at every turn, and you'll surely have good results. If you fail at any one of these, your service quality will surely suffer.

This simple acronym will assist your thinking about your everyday decisions, and it can guide your work at almost any point in time. It can affect how you will apply yourself in a meeting, how you can address a challenge, or how you complete a document. If you practice it enough, you will begin to habitually deliver a quality service. As Aristotle said, "excellence is not act;" it cannot be turned on or off but happens once we have mastered the process of doing things right. If you ever doubt the right way to respond to a customer situation, then simply *think F.A.A.S.T.*

PARTICIPATE IN THE COLLECTIVE WISDOM

"It is not once nor twice but times without number that the same ideas make their appearance in the world."

– Aristotle

WHAT IS COLLECTIVE WISDOM?

There are very few books on how to walk a tightrope. Upon research you will find most books that have something to do with tightrope walking are using it as a metaphor (like mine). This is because people don't learn to walk tightropes from a book. They are either born into the circus life, or they somehow find themselves in a situation where they are exposed to a vast array of knowledge and experience about this particular profession.

Nik Wallenda, currently the world's most successful aerialist, is a seventh generation tightrope walker. Like many tightrope walkers, his knowledge of his craft has been passed down through generations by his family in such a way that he was able to master the existing knowledge quickly and then furthered it by pushing his skills beyond previous accomplishments. Without access to such a database of knowledge, Nik would never have been able to accelerate his learning and abilities to such heights. He would have been forced to learn from his mistakes and repeat things over and over again to refine his technique and abilities. Such a mistake at the wrong time could easily prove fatal.

Instead, Nik's access to a homegrown database of best practices provided him a way to quickly learn and master the skills of his profession at a very early age. This enabled Nik to move into unchartered territories and accomplish things that no previous aerialist has achieved, such as tightrope walking directly across Niagara Falls! This database of knowledge, which has been built up over time, reused as a catalyst for learning and then extended with new achievement, is what we call *Collective Wisdom*.

The concept of using the collective wisdom to accelerate learning is not new. The world has been collecting wisdom since man learned to communicate. Primitive cultures passed on lessons learned from generation to generation by developing stories and myths and passing them down to their children. Modern cultures began keeping formal records of how they implemented procedures so that others could learn them quickly and make adjustments if more efficient alternatives became available.

In the hope of reducing engagement failure rates, service providers have discovered the value of collecting their own industry-specific wisdom. As we have discussed, repeatedly delivering customer success is difficult because each engagement is made up of different people on both sides of the engagement. The varying skill level of the individuals involved in each engagement creates huge variability with regard to how the activities in each engagement will be executed. Unlike many other professions, there is no certification of a professional service consultant's ability to deliver an engagement. There are sometimes certifications for some of the skills required, but there is none for his or her ability to deliver the entire engagement successfully. Similarly, there is no certification for a customer's ability to preside over his or her own engagements. This leaves us in a situation where the skill levels of the individuals on any given engagement are totally unpredictable.

Left unassisted, this unpredictability leads to widely varying results -- even on similar types of engagements! This kind of *crapshoot* for success is not an ideal business model for obvious reasons, so service providers assist their staff by providing them access to the lessons learned by their predecessors. By teaching their employees the lessons that led to success in prior engagements, they minimize the chance of failure in such a way that makes the business model profitable. This use of collective wisdom makes it possible for different people to work with different customers and yet achieve similar results. This interaction of people and knowledge underpins the business model that professional services firm's replicate all over the world. Professional services firms provide their customers with value by offering them the following.

PEOPLE + EXPERIENCE + RELEVANT KNOWLEDGE = PROFESSIONAL SERVICES VALUE

As you can see, *you* are an integral part of this formula. Given that you represent both the *people* and *experience* part of the equation, shouldn't you be intimately familiar with the only variable that doesn't directly relate to you? Working on an engagement and not using the full extent of your relevant knowledge is only providing the customer with two-thirds of your value.

If you are not bringing your firm's relevant knowledge to your engagement, then you are not providing the customer with the value of a professional service.

For a professional services firm, the collective wisdom represents everything it has learned about success and failure based on all prior engagements. The collective wisdom lays a path for your engagement's greatest possible chance of success. This collective wisdom, and the success it facilitates, is one of the key attributes customers use to select a service provider. This makes the collective wisdom one of the services provider's most valuable assets. Without it, the service provider is just a group of experienced people with no relevant knowledge, and customers don't want only two thirds of your potential value.

Your company's collective wisdom has enormous value, and you are entrusted with its future. It is sitting there, waiting for you to do something with it. You are more than just a part of the professional services value equation; you are the co-custodian of your company's greatest legacy. You need to be engaged with it -- not just by using it, but also by taking on the responsibility of maintaining its growth and protecting it. Use the collective wisdom to walk back and forth across the professional services tightrope, and you will cement your reputation as a career professional.

THE BENEFITS OF USING COLLECTIVE WISDOM

Collective Wisdom can be found in many forms. It can be embedded in something as small as a form, or it can be as complex as a multi-phase methodology. Once it exists, most professional services consultants see these assets as a way to more easily complete a task or process. While this is accurate, this benefit represents only the tip of the collective wisdom's overall value! When used correctly in a professional services environment, the collective wisdom provides the following additional benefits:

- It is the primary method of communicating to all employees, the best-known way to successfully deliver the service. This collective wisdom acts as a baseline so that everyone knows the right process to follow at any given time, and everyone can deliver it the same way. It allows for reliable and consistent service delivery, which is what customer and professional services firm want.

- It saves time by fast-forwarding repeatable or mundane tasks. Knowledge can be pre-built into forms, processes or even simply collected as "best practices" that can be used to avoid or minimize mistakes and significantly shorten the time to complete a process.

- It provides the ability for an organization to train its employees, partners, and customers faster and with greater quality to maximize the chances of a successful engagement. Today, some companies have collective wisdom that can teach college graduates to deliver the same level of service that required a more experienced expert many years ago.

- The ability to communicate a baseline process also provides a way to rapidly grow a services firm once it becomes successful. Without a baseline process, the growth of a professional services firm is going to meet with varying results, which will only act to hamper that growth. This situation cripples growth because every step forward results in the creation of a problem that requires another step backward. But a services process that can be reliably repeated will grow much more consistently without the frequent steps backward. This is the kind of centralized knowledge that is at the heart of all multinational large-scale service providers.

If collective wisdom is ignored, it is useless. It acts only as salt to rub into the wound of failure once you have realized that you could have used it to avoid your unfortunate outcome. This is a sobering thought and the primary reason that participating in the collective wisdom has its own principle. You cannot ignore the collective wisdom you have available to you without it coming back to bite you.

YOU AND THE COLLECTIVE WISDOM

Whether you know it or not, it is incumbent upon you to familiarize yourself with the materials that exist within your firm. You may be told where they reside or you may have been given training on it once, but the reality is that collective wisdom is always growing and changing. It has a tendency to grow and transform as your firm and the industry it serves changes. You should review your collective wisdom every time you begin a new engagement to make sure that your understanding of it is up to date. This is not only what a great professional services consultant does, but it is also what the customer expects.

A customer expects you to walk into their office at the beginning of an engagement with the combined knowledge of your entire firm -- maybe even your entire industry!

The customer expects that you are ready to provide them with services that are equal to or better than the money that they have agreed to pay your firm. If you happen to deliver something of lesser value and you did not use the collective wisdom available to you, it creates a difficult situation for you personally and for your firm for the following reasons:

- If you ignored the best practices, your customer and your firm will believe that you are not taking your role as a professional services consultant seriously. Don't put your career at risk by ignoring the collective wisdom. Even if you fail after employing the best practices, at least you know you followed the best recommendation available.

- Your company may even need to compensate the customer on the claim that they hired you precisely because of your best practices, and you failed to deliver them! This claim can be hard to refute, so the service provider may have to provide the customer with a credit or offer to do a sizable amount of work for free. Either of which upsets the balance you are trying to maintain.

Use the collective wisdom when it is available because it will help you build your career. You can always apply your unique abilities to the collective wisdom once you have gained experience with it. I love to see consultants who dig into the collective wisdom first when trying to solve customer business problems. This behavior demonstrates an attempt to maximize our value to the customer. In your current position, your firm's collective wisdom has been entrusted to you. Don't squander it. Don't try to reinvent it. You will get a chance to add to it once you have taken the time to learn and practice how to use it.

UNPREDICTABLE REACTIONS TO THE COLLECTIVE WISDOM

In all of my professional services executive roles, I have put together some form of center of excellence to collect our wisdom and then offer it to the open market. We have done this as a way of creating interest in our ability to ensure customer success. As we have discussed, there is no guarantee for success, but that should never get in the way of good marketing. The reason I do it is because customers know that they have a better chance of success if they work with a service provider who reuses their collective wisdom. Customers want service providers to help them achieve results that they are unable to achieve themselves, so advertising that you collect and reuse your secrets to success is always a good way to generate new opportunities.

That said, customers also have the potential to react negatively to collective wisdom. I have often seen large enterprise customers claim their goals are so unique that the collective wisdom brings no advantage. This can be frustrating because there is rarely, if ever, absolutely *no* value in reusing some part of your existing knowledge. It is always better to take advantage of even the smallest head start rather than starting from scratch, but I have seen customers simply dismiss this notion. To counter this, we must adopt the same technique we discussed in *Principle #2: Always Know What Done Looks Like* for *prescribing done*. When you're faced with a customer who cannot see the value the collective wisdom provides, it is similarly time to employ your expertise as a consultant and prescribe a remedy to their situation. .

FIELD EXAMPLE: PRESCRIBING THE COLLECTIVE WISDOM

Jeffrey Wells, an experienced professional services executive from Australia and one of my personal mentors, faced this very situation. He had been requested by a large airline to provide an urgent solution to handle an imminent influx of travellers. Thankfully, the solution was one that Jeff's organization had already successfully implemented elsewhere. For a variety of reasons, the airline simply felt that the collective wisdom did not apply to their unique situation. The customer believed so profoundly that they were unique that they refused to utilize the collective wisdom, despite the fact that they had an immovable deadline that was going to make a custom solution almost impossible to build. Here is how Jeffrey tells the story.

"We were engaged to design and deliver a new public facing airline check-in solution for an Australian airline client who was adamant they did not want to use an existing solution we had deployed in North America. There was an impending public event that was about to drastically increase the number of travellers going through their daily check-in process, and they knew that their current process would struggle under such high demand. With an impossibly short timeframe, approximately half of what was normally required to resolve a problem like this, the client was facing the risk of having their brand damaged by high wait times and chaos at their check-in.

Despite pulling together a global team of experts who believed in the collective wisdom we had accumulated through similar client engagements in North America, the client insisted that our proposal to reuse assets we had already built was unacceptable. For us, this was an opportune time to demonstrate our value to the client and provide them with a win in the face of such a difficult challenge, but they were not willing to listen to our advice.

To address this, we had to find a way to highlight that their needs were not dissimilar to the airlines in North America who had already deployed our system. As a part of the client's request for our proposal, we had received a list of requirements detailing their intended outcomes. Despite our initial recommendations to consider existing solutions, the client was still adamant that their needs were unique and that these solutions were not appropriate. During one of our initial sales calls, we showed a presentation where we walked through and discussed each of the requirements in detail to make sure that we fully understood them. After discussing each of them, we began to place checkmarks alongside many of the requirements. The client did ask us what these checkmarks meant, but we politely told them that we would discuss that at the end of the meeting.

After reviewing several hundred requirements, we unveiled the meaning of the check marks. Each requirement that had a checkmark was a requirement that we could satisfy by reusing the collective wisdom of the North American solution. When we counted up all of the checkmarks, we found that we had satisfied 90% of the requirements simply by reusing the assets we already had available to us.

In light of this news, the client agreed to rethink their position. Shortly thereafter, we secured the engagement and eventually delivered an entirely new check-in process to them, which also provided them with a competitive advantage in the Australian market. It also made it possible for them to deal with huge increases in traffic that this public event (the Sydney Olympics) drove through their terminals.

As a direct result of this engagement's success, we have continued to work with this client on many other engagements. Because we harnessed the power of our existing assets to achieve so much in such a short period of time, both my staff and my client's staff refer to this as one of the more satisfying engagements they have ever worked on. Despite the final solution only being 10% customized for our client, it provided them with a solution that was still customized to their specific needs. At the end of the day, this was a huge win for everyone involved."

This story is a great example of why service providers must continue to push their customers toward the best solution to their problem, even when the customer does not recognize it. Of course, there is a point at which the service provider must stop pushing, but in my experience, the problem of failing to push hard enough is more likely to lead to failed engagements. When the service provider allows the customer to talk them into acting differently than what their own experience would suggest, failure often results. The collective wisdom provides you a great way to demonstrate to a customer that your previous experience can be applied to their current situation, despite how unique they feel it is. When correctly applied, employing this will yield a far better result and a longer-term relationship with the customer.

CONTRIBUTING TO THE COLLECTIVE WISDOM

An often-overlooked element of the *Collective Wisdom* is the important premise that every professional services consultant should not only use it, but they must also contribute to it. Too often, companies let the professional services consultants think that advancing the collective wisdom must be left to those in the center of excellence, or to those who have seniority. This frustrates me. Any individual who has learned their craft well and can understand the concepts in this book has the ability to advance the collective wisdom, not only of their company, but also of their professional services field of expertise.

Some companies recognize this and pay their consultants for the creation of new materials. While I agree with this practice, I also believe that when a services organization creates the right culture, the growth of the collective wisdom does not require money as a catalyst. Rather, it occurs naturally because the company clearly articulates to its employees that they are trusted not only as users of the collective wisdom but also as the custodians responsible for furthering it.

Once you have gained experience with your collective wisdom, feel free to question and challenge it. If you can find another way to achieve better results, you should propose it. Of course, you should always discuss these changes with your manager and get approval before deploying them. Your manager will help you determine if the changes are likely to work. If your improvements are accepted, then you should take pride in the fact that you just enhanced the collective wisdom.

Each services organization should have a well-defined repository for its collective wisdom. If an individual consultant does not know where to go to find it, then the collective wisdom will never be used. There should also be a clearly defined process for accessing, reusing and contributing to the collective wisdom. Those who reuse it and contribute to it should be acknowledged. Not every suggested improvement will be valid, but every attempt should be acknowledged and treated with respect. If this can be done, then the collective value of a professional services organization will grow rapidly. As a professional services consultant, you have every right to expect this from your employer. The collective wisdom is what makes services companies valuable. If you cannot access your collective wisdom, or you are unable to contribute to it, then you should raise this to your management team immediately.

AN INTRODUCTION TO INTELLECTUAL PROPERTY

The concept of Intellectual Property is complicated, and the law that governs it can quickly become confusing. More importantly, I am not a lawyer, so I will not provide any specific legal advice on the subject. Nevertheless, a company's IP is often its most valuable asset and the collective wisdom you work with every day constitutes the lion's share of it. Your company already spends a lot of money trying to keep it safe by employing lawyers to negotiate its ownership, lodge patents with it, and securing it from theft and misuse. As a custodian with almost unlimited access to this collective wisdom, I believe that you must know the basics of how to identify and protect it. For that reason, I have summarized the concept of IP so that you can effectively recognize what it is, why it is so valuable, and how you can help protect it. This is for the sake of your employer and your career. Losing or misusing your company's intellectual property could turn out to be a disaster and cause significant problems for you. For that fact alone, read on.

What is Intellectual Property?

If you haven't picked up on it, the terms *Collective Wisdom*, *Know-how* and *Intellectual Property (IP)* are used somewhat interchangeably. While I can provide you with the formal definition that IP is *"the accumulated know-how used to create,"* it is sometimes difficult to identify and define. For a professional services firm specifically, the collective wisdom we have been discussing is going to make up a large part of your firm's total intellectual property.

For the purpose of an example, let's consider IP in the context of a recipe for *cakes* (yes, cakes, follow me for a moment if you will). When a cake is baked, it represents the outcome of successfully applying a specific recipe containing both raw ingredients and a process. The recipe is the know-how required to take those raw ingredients and produce the cake so that it tastes a specific way. When a customer buys the cake, he is paying for the value of the recipe's outcome, not the recipe. Similarly, he now owns the cake and can do whatever he likes with it, but he has no right to own the recipe that created it. While the customer pays a market rate for the cake, the value of the recipe is exponentially larger because it represents the ability to repeat the process of making the same cake. It is exponential because no one can possibly know how many cakes the market may want to buy in the future, and the baker who invented and owns the recipe has the right to reuse it as long as he or she wants.

This analogy works because you are selling a kind of recipe similar to that of a cake. The outcome of your recipe, however, is your *customer's success.* Your firm owns that recipe, and it is allowing you to use it while you work there as an employee. Almost everything you do on an engagement uses or reuses some portion of that recipe. Every document you create, every plan that you build, every spreadsheet you provide, and every piece of code you deliver contains some of the know-how your firm provided to you for the purposes of delivering customer success. This also includes any process you follow such as a methodology or a best practice.

The concept of IP is complicated because it is both intangible and of high value. IP is the measurable, yet intangible, know-how that makes it possible for us to create tangible work products that may have commercial value. This includes documents we produce and the procedures we execute, and it extends to almost anything you can imagine that you might deliver to your customer. They all require know-how to be created. As the production of these tangible work products are born from the application of intangible know-how, the final work product itself is considered to have two separate components of value:

1. *The Cake.* The first component is the tangible work product itself (e.g.: the cake, a document, a computer program) and the contents within it. For a service provider, this may be a description of how to implement a

process, or it may be a customer specific document such as a project plan or a design specification.

2. *The Recipe.* The second component is the intangible IP that is inherent within the document (e.g.: the structured process of creation). This is the know-how that the service provider applied to create the tangible work product. The know-how may be obvious in the work product, but it may also be invisible. Regardless, it is considered to be a part of the tangible work product.

The intangible know-how in these work products may be deliberately or accidentally transferred to others in a variety of ways (e.g.: spoken word, process manual, through the deconstruction of the work product). Once transferred, it can be difficult to discern who has the right to continue using this know-how for the creation of future tangibles products and services of value. For this reason, the law provides us the ability to protect IP, and it also provides us the right to buy and sell it as an asset. This transfer of IP ownership gives the assigned owner the right to continue using the IP for the creation of future work products. If IP is accidentally transferred, the owner loses control of how it gets distributed. Once that happens, other people may begin using and the real owner is no longer the sole beneficiary of that know-how. While illegal, it may be possible for other companies to rebrand that know-how and then use it to win business against the original owner. The potential lost revenue from losing or accidentally transferring IP can be significant.

Hence, a professional services contract usually deals with the tangible and intangible components separately. For the tangible work product, the service provider may or may not grant ownership to the customer. So long as the customer is not planning or able to derive income from the commercial use of the work product, I am usually ok with the customer being granted this ownership. Some service providers may differ in their approach, and to be fair, I can argue the case both ways. However, for the intangible IP, it is always recommended that service providers retain all of the IP brought to and *acquired from* the engagement. It is important that the service provider retains the IP acquired from the engagement; otherwise, it is impossible to accumulate it over time, and if a service provider's collective wisdom is not growing, their market value may stagnate.

Before investigating the real value of IP a little further, let's summarize this section by making it clear that your employer is providing you with access to know-how that you are using to assist customers in achieving successful outcomes. While that know-how may be inherent within the work products of your engagement, the ownership of the work product and its IP are treated separately. You need to be aware how each of these assets is being treated on your engagement.

So What's the Big Deal?

To understand the real value of IP, let's return to the cake and its recipe. As we have discussed, when a customer buys a cake, he does not buy any ownership in the recipe for that cake. However, suppose that the customer really likes this cake and buys it regularly. At some point, he starts to think how wonderful it would be to have the recipe for himself. Then, he could make the cakes whenever he wanted and not have to pay the baker anything. He could also resell any cakes he doesn't need for whatever price he likes. The customer offers the baker the price of 1,000 cakes to buy the recipe. The customer thinks this is a fair price to pay for the ownership of the recipe because it is so much more than the price he pays for just one cake. If the baker sells the recipe to the customer, she will no longer have the right to use it, so her business will then be limited to whatever other recipes she has that could generate revenue.

The offer sounds reasonable to the baker, but to double check, she does some quick math. She currently sells 100 of these cakes a week at a 25% profit, which means that the customer's offer would represent 40 weeks of income (100 x 25% = 25 cakes of income per week divided into the 1,000 cakes offered as a purchase price for the recipe). If the owner sold her recipe, she would be accelerating 40 weeks of profits but losing the potential value of selling the cakes forever. If the baker is reliant on the income from the cakes, this is not a good deal. To give some order of magnitude to the situation, let's assume the baker was counting on building her retirement from the cake profits over the next 10 years. At today's pricing (not accounting for the effects of market variations and inflation), she would need to sell the recipe for 13,000 times the value of just one cake to earn the same profits (25 cakes profit per week x 52 weeks a year x 10 years).

This illustrates that the value of the product created by the know-how pales in comparison to the value of the knowhow that created it. This is why IP is so valuable. Everything you do in professional services relates to your knowhow. You have no physical product to sell other than your ability to take a customer's business problem and apply your knowhow to solve it. IP is therefore the lifeblood of a professional services firm.

For a services firm, intellectual property is likely to be its most valuable asset. It is being entrusted to you. How you use it, protect it and contribute to it is going to be a measure of your success.

How to Protect Intellectual Property

Because of IP's considerable importance to the professional services firm, I believe it is essential that all consultants in the field be adequately trained in how to protect it. Failure to adequately protect IP can result in an accidental transfer or otherwise lead to its misuse in a way that de-values your firm's business. As a professional services consultant and custodian of your company's collective wisdom, you should charge yourself with these tasks.

- Introduce yourself to your company's legal representative. Tell him or her that you would like a copy of the company's standard services agreement so that you can familiarize yourself with the legal framework under which you provide your services.

- Read through your company's services agreements. Understand their standard view of intellectual property. Be prepared to talk to customers about the fact that your company retains all of its IP rights in the intellectual property it creates and begin identifying the IP assets you have access to.

- Talk to your manager if you think customers, ex-employees, competitors or partners are incorrectly reusing intellectual property.

- Talk to your manager if you think intellectual property is not being protected correctly within your company.

- Protect (both physically and electronically) any asset that you think may contain IP (e.g.: process documents, forms, best practices, methodologies etc.).

- Take data protection training if your company offers it. It is usually a short course taking only a couple of hours of your time. This may be offered as a part of your company's certification to some security standard such as SOC2, but if you ask your HR or training department, they will be able to tell you if it is available. This training will give you knowledge on the following topics:

o How to identify different types of data that may need protecting;

o How to securely prevent access to important data;

o How to safely transmit important data;

Protecting and expanding a service provider's IP is critical to retaining its long-term value. Understanding what constitutes IP and knowing your responsibility to help protect it are very important. It not only helps you understand how to do your job, but it also aids your ability to develop a career within the industry. Remember, you have been entrusted with your company's most valuable asset, and you should be sure to use that sobering fact as an incentive to stay vigilant about its protection.

CHAPTER SUMMARY

A tightrope walker must absorb the age-old wisdom and techniques that have been passed from one generation of performers to the next. The specific know-how created by one generation is made available to the next so that they can quickly achieve the same success by learning to avoid the costly mistakes that others have already encountered. This gives every subsequent generation a head start that, if used wisely, gives them the opportunity to achieve more than their predecessors.

Similarly, every professional services firm contains collective wisdom that must be passed on from one generation of employees to the next. The time necessary to learn the process of delivering customer success has been condensed so that you can quickly learn it. You must choose if you are going to seize the opportunity to further enhance the wisdom around you or to waste it. Whatever you decide, it is likely to determine your long-term value to your employer and your customer. Collective wisdom is the heart and soul of delivering professional services and becoming a champion of it will serve your career greatly.

STAY ENGAGED

"The biggest mistake that you can make is to believe that you are working for somebody else. Job security is gone. The driving force of a career must come from the individual. Remember: Jobs are owned by the company, you own your career!"

– Earl Nightingale

YOU ONLY HAVE ONE CAREER

A tightrope walker cannot lose his concentration for a single second. If he does, his career may be over—not to mention his life! He must remain calm and think clearly regardless of any distractions. Overreacting or failing to adjust to an environmental change could spell disaster. This intense concentration, coupled with astute decision-making, gives the tightrope walker the best possible chance of crossing the wire safely.

While fortunately less fatal and less intense, it is important that you apply the same techniques to your professional services career. There are many books on this topic and many names for the attitude you must have to successfully manage your own career. I (and many others) call it *staying engaged*, and it is the act of consistently considering your career status and the direction you want to take it. Fail to do this, and you will lose sight of where you are headed and leave the direction of your career in the hands of others. This principle focuses in on what it means to stay engaged with a professional services career. It is a mix of professional services specific and good-old career advice that should be followed no matter your field of expertise. The goal is to give you the tools you need to adequately focus and assess your own career so that you can determine your own future.

I have seen consultants with great potential leave a job only to see their careers stagnate, but I've also seen others leave and have their careers flourish. The latter is very satisfying, and I try my hardest to make sure that when a consultant wants to leave my team, he or she considers the elements of this principle. The worst thing that a consultant can do is falsely think that their employer is out to get them and decide to move on, when the reality is, it can be their own lack of engagement causing the problem.

This issue is easily resolved, and it shouldn't drive someone to leave a good job. If you' re unable to recognize that you have disengaged from the company and the effect it is having on your job satisfaction, then the situation is likely to repeat itself at your next job. So instead of furthering your career, the move only serves to stagnate it. In order to make sure that you are accurately assessing your own career, be sure to stay engaged.

To be clear, this principle is not promoting that you should stay at your current job, nor is it suggesting that you go out job hunting. Instead, it is giving you information and a set of tools to objectively assess your career situation. What you do once you have obtained this clarity is entirely up to you.

Most of us only have one career, so it is important to maintain its health. What we have done in the past writes the ticket for our future and someday, we hope to look back on our career and feel satisfied that it was worth the time and effort it consumed.

While we would all agree that a consultant should never leave a good job, the reality is that few people know how to accurately assess their own circumstance in order to make an informed decision. While many employers do not sufficiently recognize or reward some of their individuals, it is also true that employees can sometimes exaggerate the impact their employer is having on their own discontentment. This is because it can just be easier to blame someone else for how you feel about your job. *Staying engaged* will help you avoid incorrectly deciding to move to another employer before determining if you have maximized the opportunities you have at your current one. After all, an unsuccessful job move will be a waste of your time, so give your current employer a fair shot at making you happy and successful.

Although you may think this situation will never happen to you, the reality is that sometimes the mindset that drives people to leave a job is beyond their control. Being overworked, being chased by another employer, not receiving a promotion or not receiving an expected salary increase can all affect your state of mind when making a career decision. To prevent this situation, it is important to adopt this principle and the techniques within it.

THE GENERIC PROFESSIONAL SERVICES CAREER MAP

What does a career in professional services look like? More importantly, what will *your* career in professional services look like? Where are you today in your career and where are you heading? These are important questions that you should be able to answer, yet I'm guessing you do not contemplate them enough, nor are you talking directly to your manager about them. One of the reasons may be that it is sometimes difficult to visualize what a professional services career might look like. This problem is compounded by the fact that a lot of professional services managers do not have a precise concept of what a professional services career path looks like either. Heck, I didn't really think about it in detail until I was in my mid-thirties.

To that end, I present to you the *Generic Professional Services Career Map*. After having guided hundreds of different individuals through their professional services careers, I have developed this map as a way to help individuals understand their career options. It is based on my experience in the delivery of information technology and software professional services, but I have worked hard to adapt it generically to almost any type of professional service. It is not intended as a hard and fast template but more of a guide that should be detailed enough to help you identify where you want to go and how you may be able to get there.

By way of introduction, the generic professional services career map makes the assumption that each individual is seeking to progress his or her career forward or at least laterally (sideways). The desire and urgency to progress one's career will vary from individual to individual, and it may even vary wildly at different points within an individual's career. Therefore, the map is designed to highlight the various potential career paths an individual may take; it also identifies some of the potential challenges one may encounter therein. Because we all progress in our careers at different speeds, there is no mention of an expected number of months or years it should take for someone to progress across each stage. However, the map does indicate the core attributes a services firm is looking for in its consultants at each particular stage of their career, so it gives you the ability to objectively assess your own readiness. You should ensure that the key skills I have identified for each stage align with those of your employer. While I believe they will, there is no point chasing my recommendation if your firm is looking for something different.

How to Read the Career Map

The generic professional services career map should be read from left to right. Each vertical column represents a stage of maturity within a professional services career and the white boxes represent the job roles typically available in that stage. The professional services job roles that begin with an asterisk (*) represent good entry-level positions for people breaking into the industry or leaving school with a suitable qualification for that professional services firm's area of expertise. The greyed boxes, while not an exhaustive list, represent good transition points out of the professional services arena into some other closely related field.

The black barriers between each career stage represent the increasing level of difficulty that a professional services consultant will encounter in trying to move from one stage to the next. The further the career progression, the harder it becomes to break into the next stage. Rather than forward progress, the chart also assumes that a consultant can move up or down within a particular stage, which equates to a *lateral* career move.

The horizontal lines between each role within a stage are purposefully equivalent to the black column that represents the effort required to move through the "Decision Making Divide." This is because the effort required for a consultant to move laterally is equivalent to the effort required to move from the *Competent* to *Decisive* career stage. The significance of this is that once you have made it into (or past) the *Competent Stage*, you may find that lateral moves begin to look easier to you than forward progress. Don't let this bother you. Sometimes, moving laterally can open up your next move, particularly if it makes it easier for you to demonstrate the core attributes expected in that next stage.

The horizontal *Operational Chasm* has a unique feature in that it is almost completely a one-way divide. Individuals who start on a Technical Path can sometimes (with varying success) cross into an Operational Path if they show an aptitude for running the day-to-day business operations of a services team. The reverse, however, is rarely true. Individuals seldom cross from the operational side to the technical side because of the huge skills gap required to be effective in the Technical Path. Passing from the Operational Path to the Technical Path is not impossible but highly improbable until Stage 5 when technical capabilities become irrelevant.

Before we dig into each of the career stages, please review the map and acquaint yourself with the general ideas that it is presenting. Namely, that as a career progresses from its early stages, the barriers are relatively small and the number of opportunities tends to broaden. At some point in the middle of a career, the number tends to decrease, and the barriers to reach them become larger. Review this map in light of your own experience for a few moments before continuing.

GENERIC PROFESSIONAL SERVICES CAREER MAP

>> STAGES OF CAREER GROWTH OVER TIME >>

KEY TO ROLES
- Services Roles
- * Entry Level Services Roles
- Services Exit Points

Stages: 1. POTENTIAL | 2. COMPETENT | 3. DECISIVE (Product or Development) | 4. LEADER (Product or Development) | 5. RESULTS | 6. RELIABLE

Divides / Chasms: COMPETENCY DIVIDE (between 1 & 2) · DECISION MAKING DIVIDE (between 2 & 3) · LEADERSHIP CHASM (between 3 & 4) · RESULTS CHASM (between 4 & 5) · RELIABILITY CHASM (between 5 & 6)

TECHNICAL CAREER PATH

1. POTENTIAL	2. COMPETENT	3. DECISIVE (Product or Development)	4. LEADER (Product or Development)	5. RESULTS	6. RELIABLE
* Field / Customer Support	Support Specialist	Senior Support Specialist	Senior Support Manager	Business Manager	
* Associate Consultant	General Consultant	Senior General Consultant	Practice Lead Consultant		
		Subject Mattae Expert Consultant	Industry Expert		
		Architect	Senior Architect		
		Technical Presales	Senior Technical Presales		
	Trainer	Senior Trainer	Training Manager	Business Manager	
* Document Writer	Senior Document Writer	Curriculum Developer	Curriculum Specialist		
* Test Script Writer	Tester	QA Specialist	QA Manager		
	Technical Project Manager	Senior Technical Project Manager			EXECUTIVE LEADERSHIP

OPERATIONS CAREER PATH

OPERATIONS CHASM (between 3 & 4)

1. POTENTIAL	2. COMPETENT	3. DECISIVE	4. LEADER	5. RESULTS	6. RELIABLE
* Associate Business Analyst	Business Analyst	Project Manager	Senior Project Manager	Business Manager	
* Operations Support Analyst	* Operations Analyst	Senior Operations Analyst	Services Presales		
			Operations Manager		
	Other Divisional Operations Roles	Other Divisional Operations Roles	Other Divisional Management Roles	Other Divisional Management Roles	EXECUTIVE LEADERSHIP

THE PROFESSIONAL SERVICES CAREER STAGES

The professional services career map is useful because it tells you a lot about how to progress your career; it may also tell you a little about your career history. To begin, each stage is named after the key attribute a services firm is looking for you to master before you are eligible to be promoted into that stage. To exit your current stage, you should be looking at the stage ahead and identifying the ways that you can demonstrate your mastery of that specific skill.

Stage 1: Potential

Employers are looking for recruits that have *potential*. This book is not about landing your first job, but almost all companies hiring entry-level positions are trying to identify candidates that are articulate, smart, and genuinely enthusiastic about their area of expertise. Albeit unscientific, it is reasonable to assume a professional services firm's equation for an ideal Stage 1 candidate is something like this: *potential = articulation + smarts + enthusiasm*. Once you've entered this stage, an individual can exit it by demonstrating that they are *competent* in the areas relevant to the services being provided. To cross the Competency Divide, an individual must demonstrate that they have aligned themselves with the company's expectation of the current job role, and that they are able to reliably execute it to an acceptable standard. At this stage, it is easier to progress to Stage 2 than it is to move laterally to another Stage 1 job.

Stage 2: Competent

In Stage 2, you are expected to demonstrate competence to the point of being able to achieve business outcomes without guidance. You are expected to know your craft and execute company policies and procedures like a professional. Now that you are competent, it is as easy to exit this stage as to change jobs within it. This is because moving laterally usually only requires one or two additional different technical skills in order for you to fulfill another job function. This can sometimes be easier than learning the soft skills required to progress to the next stage.

If you are finding that your skill set is more business focused than the specific technical skills you require to work with your customers, then this stage presents a good opportunity for you to move into the *Operations Career Path.* This move allows you to focus more on the operational planning and delivery of your team's services rather than understanding how to actually deliver a successful engagement. While leaving the technical career path can be a great decision for some people, you must understand that once you have left it behind, the technical career path can be difficult to re-enter. Employers are looking for people with current and refined technical skills, and once yours begin to atrophy, they become less likely to be the reason for which you are employed.

During this stage, you should look ahead to Stage 3 where the key skill for entry is decisiveness. Your firm is almost always looking for people to move into this next stage because a team full of good decision-makers is a real asset in a business where employees have direct contact with its customers. To cross the Decision-Making divide, you must demonstrate that you are self-sufficient in your day-to-day actions and that you can deal with difficult customer situations early and well. Essentially, you must show that you have a reasonable grasp of all the principles outlined in this book. Once beyond Stage 2, you begin to cement yourself as an experienced professional services consultant.

Stage 3: Decisive
Once you have made it to Stage 3, you are expected to be able to execute at a level that facilitates successful outcomes in the face of adversity. When challenged by a difficult situation,

you will be expected to own and resolve situations that arise within your day-to-day activities through peer communication and consultation. This is the heart of the professional services career. Because of the depth of skills required to exit this stage, you may find yourself within this stage for much longer than the previous ones. During this stage you may even find that lateral moves are an attractive option as you try different roles in preparation for moving across the Leadership Chasm. The barrier between this stage and the next is now a *chasm* rather than a *divide* because as the chart indicates, the number of opportunities available within the next stage is fewer, and only a small number of people within a firm are promoted across it each year.

As a side note, this stage also helps explain that a career path is in reality three-dimensional. Many people spend their entire careers within this stage by continuing to develop deeper and deeper technical skills within one role. It is possible for someone to be perfectly happy becoming more and more of an expert without progressing across career stages. Hence, they may find no need to progress out of this stage at all.

To exit this stage, you must be able to demonstrate *leadership*. Leadership can mean different things to different organizations, but essentially, it means that you are able to make sound decisions that others can follow. Similarly, you are able to affect the decision-making of others in a positive way, or you are able to positively impact the decision-making process of the team around you. Taking the skill of decision-making and turning it into leadership is not easy. There are plenty of resources on the topic of leadership, and it is best for you to begin researching it well before trying to exit this stage. Remember to try and find a style of leadership that suits you, and avoid copying the styles of those around you. Forcing yourself into a leadership style that doesn't suit you will undermine your success.

To prepare to cross this chasm, you may want to start mentoring younger Stage 1 employees or even assist with their onboarding. This will help you build and demonstrate leadership potential. You could also run a small cross-functional project where you can demonstrate your abilities to lead peers in other groups to achieve a common goal. If you are trying to exit this stage, then spend some time thinking about ways you can demonstrate your leadership skills and talk to your manager about being able to put some of your time towards it.

Stage 4: Leader

You are now a leader. You are most likely still in the field, so we sometimes refer to this stage of maturity as *field leadership*. At this point in time, you are asked to be somewhat of a player-coach. You are probably being asked to complete a functional role while also owning the general quality of that role across the entire team. For example, you might be a project manager, but you may also be responsible for the skills development of the whole project management team. This role can sometimes be called a *Practice Lead or a Practice Manager*.

Getting out of Stage 3 was hard, but getting out of Stage 4 is even harder because there are fewer Stage 5 people needed. This is simply the economics of a hierarchical business. As you move up the hierarchy, there are less and less roles that you are capable of filling. To exit this phase, the company is looking for an individual to demonstrate the ability to own and operate a part of the business. This is called the *Ownership Chasm* because you will cross it once you show an ability to own the business environment around you. This is more than just leadership. It is leadership *plus the ownership* of obtaining business results.

This means you'll be responsible for keeping to budget, hitting revenue numbers, hiring and firing talent, understanding business scale, and a myriad of other business practices. As you can see, the skills required are becoming more business oriented, rather than you current area of subject matter expertise. This is again one of the reasons why people who are not comfortable with this kind of progress may dig deeper into their existing technical capabilities and utilize the third-dimension of career progress.

For each company, the right mixture of skills to enter Stage 5 will vary, so it is important that you know exactly what your company wishes to see from you in order to move into the fifth stage. Often, this may be something like taking on a special project or a vendor-selection process. During such an exercise, you should look to understand the operating functions of the services business in greater detail. This means understanding elements of the business that may include time card collection, resource assignment, contract negotiation, or financial operations.

Stage 5: Results

Welcome to *middle management*. In this stage, the individual owns the business results that the team is delivering. This may be for a part of the professional services business, or it may be for the whole professional services division. By this stage, the relevance of your original career path has waned significantly. While subject matter expertise can still be valuable, it is clearly not needed from a business manager on a day-to-day basis. A technical background can still have an advantage in understanding the hurdles your team faces, particularly when you're asking them to work harder or conquer a difficult challenge.

Exiting this stage is very difficult because there are now only a handful of people in your company in the Senior Management or Executive Leadership positions, and they may plan to remain there a while. You should always be willing to wait for these kinds of opportunities. However, as with any other stage, you always have the option to resign and move elsewhere if an opportunity presents itself. Your success will largely depend on how patient you are and how much you enjoy working with your current employer. Becoming impatient at this stage can harm your career. It is easy for you to think that you could move elsewhere and get a promotion to stage 6, but in most cases, stage 5 managers transfer jobs laterally. This is because stage 6 managers are expected to have already proven their ability to repeat success, and employers look for a strong track record of experience when hiring them. The decision to wait at your current company or move laterally to another company is very difficult, and you should consider it carefully.

Stage 6: Reliable

This stage is about getting *reliable results*. You can achieve these results because you understand the professional services business in great depth. Companies will hire you as a senior manager or executive under the premise that you have already had experience achieving the kind of results they aspire to. Once you have proven that you can successfully run a services business, potential employers will believe that you have the formula for success worked out. If you can convince them that you know it, they will give you the opportunity to repeat it again. Once in this stage, you have a depth of experience and *reliability* that companies will pay good money for.

From here, the professional services career can go in multiple directions. A professional services executive may simply continue to do this kind of position for twenty or more years. He or she may move around from company to company and take on challenges that appeal to them. He or she may move into larger and larger companies as a way to find more and more of a challenge. Another option may be to start his or her own professional services firm and become the owner rather than an executive who reports into a larger company. Once you have made it to this stage, there is little guidance you will obtain from this book. You should instead, begin to use your own journey as a way to inspire others to achieve the same results.

Summary: The Generic Professional Services Career Map

Thinking ahead and knowing your options will always help your chances of success. This map is designed to give you a sense of direction and to let you know what to expect as you build your professional services career. Just like delivering professional services, advancing your career requires balance. You need to spend time learning each of the stages and gaining experience at the highest level you can within it. At the same time, you don't want to stagnate in one stage too long, unless of course you are looking to dive deeper into a specific stage.

Take the time to master each stage properly. The skills you will master in each stage will get tested in subsequent stages and weaknesses will be exposed. It is better to conquer a stage entirely than to leave it prematurely and find, later, that you do not have what it takes to continue your career progression.

Not wanting to progress across the career map is OK. Career progression brings added responsibility, and this can mean longer hours, more stress, and more scrutiny of the results you achieve. Some people are more interested in the increased amount of detail and expert knowledge required by digging deeper into a particular subject matter. Just remember that it is your career, and you can make of it whatever you decide.

ENGAGING WITH YOUR CAREER

A successful career does not happen by accident. If it is going to thrive, it requires constant care and nurturing. You don't accidentally earn a promotion. The people who think about and discuss their next career steps with their managers are often the ones that get promoted. Most people earn their promotion long before the opportunity actually becomes available by displaying the necessary skills in advance of that job position opening. Why else would you get selected to fill an open position?

If you have not displayed the necessary skills to satisfy the job requirements, then you are unlikely to be selected as the best candidate. You can only be prepared for this situation if you are engaged to the point of constantly talking with your manager about the skills required for you to take the next step. Do you know what your next role will be within your current organization? Have you discussed it with your manager and agreed on the necessary skills you should demonstrate to be eligible for that move? Have you talked with your manager about who would be a good replacement for you when you move on?

Staying engaged with your career means that you know the answers to these questions. To consider yourself *engaged*, you must be engaged in the following activities:

Participate in the Collective Wisdom

There is no need to repeat the skill that has an entire principle dedicated to it, except to say that participating in the collection and growth of your company's collective wisdom is a significant factor in distinguishing yourself as a person ready for promotion.

Know Your Market Value

Know the market value of your skills by researching open positions in the market, but you should also understand that attaining this value is likely to be delayed by circumstances beyond your control. As previously discussed, having the skills and experience to fulfill a job is independent of that position being open and ready for you to fill it. While you can widen your options by continuing to look at the open market, you must also remember that people who frequently "job hop" may look suspect to prospective employers.

Knowing your market value is simply about keeping yourself informed, and if a discrepancy exists between what you're making and what you should be making, then you should know it. If there is a big difference between these two numbers, you should have that conversation with your manager and see if he or she agrees. While a salary increase can be a good incentive to leave a company, it is a mistake to chase minor salary increases. Money is not always the silver bullet for the lack of career progressions. There is a lot more to a successful career than money, and one of them is longevity, especially in senior positions.

At times, you will receive a promotion or a raise that will align your market value with your current salary, but this equilibrium does not last long. Your market value will soon again be ahead of your salary as you increase your knowledge and experience. You must be aware and be patient of the fact that your salary almost always trails your market value.

Have an Active Career Plan

Create a 12-month and a 5-year career goal. Discuss them with your manager at least once a month. Even if your manager does not bring it up, you can. Make sure the two plans are aligned. The 12-month plan must help you reach the next step towards your 5-year goal.

Don't fret about a 5-year goal being very vague. The objective is not to create a detailed vision but to create a guiding beacon to make sure that the decisions you make now are aligned with your long-term desires. Have an immediate training plan. What do you need to learn tomorrow so that you can fulfill your 12-month plan? While training can be costly, most companies underutilize their training budgets, so don't be afraid to ask for an opportunity that will enhance your success. Additionally, you can learn a great deal for free by shadowing other people or being invited to sit in on other people's meetings. Remember, you will not attain your career goals if you are not continuing to add new and relevant skills.

Know What "Success" Looks Like

Just like delivering an engagement, it is important that you have a clear definition of your own success. Know the measurable business objectives (MBO's) or key performance indicators (KPI's) your firm has assigned to you and have a plan for how you intend on achieving them. These may determine how you will get paid, and they will ultimately determine how your management team views you as an individual contributor. Staying engaged with these will help you maximize your bonuses, which will also provide you with the greatest chance of career progress when new opportunities arise.

Avoid Burnout

Working too hard and becoming disillusioned with your company is a death knell. You become bitter and close-minded, and it is almost impossible for you to see your company in a positive light. I have seen so many people go through this process, and it seldom ends well. These people are just like you. They work hard. They put in everything they have. Even if they are achieving results and getting recognition for their effort, the job still wears them down, and their attitude becomes sour. Many consultants get themselves into this situation because they believe it is a sign of weakness to admit that they are suffering from burnout.

Burnout is NOT a sign of weakness. It is a sign that something in your work-life balance is out of place. EVERYONE has a point at which burnout begins to affect their ability to be successful. The sooner you can identify it, the sooner you can repair the damage it is causing.

Burnout can cause a consultant to become petty and pick at the little thing as if they were major faults with the customer or their firm. The next thing you know, the consultant thinks that the firm is completely ignoring and underappreciating them. In most situations, this is simply fatigue talking. Sometimes, the perception may be correct; the company may be under-appreciating the individual. However, this evaluation should not be made while exhausted. My recommendation to individuals in this situation is to get some rest, recover, and get their energy back. With a clear mind, they can assess their situation without the negativity that burnout creates. This results in a much better decision-making process.

The truth is that both you and your firm need to be responsible for avoiding burnout. The firm must be aware of the amount of effort you are putting into your customer engagements and the impact it is having on your ability to be effective. You must understand that it is your personal strength of character (dedication and commitment) that is driving you to work so hard.

Burned out employees tend to leave organizations because they blame the company for working them too hard. Yet upon arriving at the next company, their work ethic drives them to continue to work hard, and the process begins to repeat itself. Don't just convince yourself that you need a change simply because you work too hard. Be sure that you draw clear work-life boundaries, and that when you begin to feel the effects of burnout, you should discuss it with your manager. It is likely that both of you will need to make some adjustments. Your manager is unlikely to want to lose you, so he or she will be motivated to help you.

Attend Company Meetings

It can feel *very* lonely in the field, so this is a small but important activity that has a large impact on your ability to stay engaged. Don't isolate yourself in the field with insufficient or incorrect information. I often find that when I am talking to an individual who is suffering from burnout, misinterpreted company decisions are one of the root causes of their discontentment. These topics are usually covered in-depth at weekly team meetings or monthly company meetings, but the individual who is burning out is usually too busy to attend them.

This is a mistake. While customer success is important, your peace of mind and knowledge of your firm is far more important. These meetings typically contain valuable information about the decisions being made around you, and they are designed to keep the field in touch with what is happening with the rest of the firm. Not to mention that these meetings often have a Q&A session, so if you missed them then you have missed your opportunity to ask clarifying questions directly to the executives.

Engage With Those Around You

Give feedback to your peers and executives in a controlled and structured manner. Do it person to person. Do it as an observation (not a criticism), and in some instances, be prepared to be wrong. Don't just drop the issue in someone's lap; come prepared with an answer or with a donation of your time to collaborate and find a mutually agreeable solution to the issue. These interactions are invaluable to your career. They demonstrate an interest in your greater surroundings and that you care about your firm's business as a whole, even if the observation is wrong.

Never go into a discussion like this with all guns blazing. As someone looking to move up in the company, this type of attitude may set you back more than it helps. Also, be aware of the "smartest person in the room" syndrome. Inexperienced people who constantly tell their peers or managers that they know how to fix everything tend to isolate themselves as ill-suited for leadership. For the most part, if you can control your own temperament in conversations like this and be calm and constructive (just like the conversations you have with your customers), then you will clearly demonstrate your value to those around you.

Learning – Having Fun – Recognition

Above all other topics, this is potentially the most important. Are you learning? Are you having fun? Are you being recognized for your successes? If your company is delivering you a positive experience in these areas, then it may be a great place for you to be, even if you are not progressing in your career. Happiness at work is critically important. Sometimes, the added headaches of career progression are not worth losing the happiness you've already found in your current position.

Most industry surveys point to at least one of these three factors as being the number one reason why employees stay or leave companies, so don't sacrifice them unnecessarily. They have real value, and if you find a place that works for you, it may be worth staying there even if you need to wait around for new opportunities, or even if you end up missing out on a few promotions. A happy work environment is not something you should give up easily as it can have a tremendous impact on your overall quality of life.

Remember, Employment is a Mutual Agreement

While you may spend a lot of time contemplating whether your job is a good fit for you, rest assured your employer is contemplating whether you are a good fit for your job. This is what managers are paid to do. Keep the *engaged* people in the right jobs and move or exit the *disengaged* people as soon as possible. If you are demonstrating active disengagement, then your manager may have plans to move you to another position or even out the door sooner than you think.

Most management teams regularly review their top and bottom performers. This process ensures that top performers are recognized and those at the bottom are rotated into other jobs, or rotated out of the company entirely. If you are disengaged, this sends a strong signal to your manager that you are not aligned with the rest of the team. As the captain of your team, your manager is paid to hire and fire in such a way to build the strongest team possible. For that reason, you must remember to demonstrate your value as a member of that team.

Summary: Engaging With Your Career

The components I have just outlined drive the level of engagement you have with your firm and your career. Consider them regularly and talk to your manager about them. If you are highly engaged, let your manager know. If you are becoming disengaged, review this maintenance list and identify what is causing your lack of engagement. Then develop an action plan with your manager. If you signal that you want to correct the disengagement that has set in then it will be in your manager's best interest to help you get re-engaged.

The value of your career will be determined by the effort you put into engaging it. That doesn't mean that you have to sacrifice family time or other personal goals to achieve success, but more that you pay attention to what matters and devote time to the maintenance of your career as a priority.

Having implemented programs that measure and track employee engagement, I can vouch that these actions will dramatically improve the satisfaction that any individual can extract from his or her job. If you employ them, it will give you the ability to constantly review whether or not your current position is good for your career or whether or not it may be better to move on.

UNDERSTANDING SALARY INCREASES

Although it is not always the primary reason people stay in a job, salary is still very important, and the process is sometimes shrouded in mystery, which can be frustrating. But even when salaries are presented in an open process, not receiving one can be just as frustrating. Not getting a salary increase often kick starts the process of your disengagement, so it is well worth knowing how to deal with it.

The Salary Adjustment Process

Almost every salary increase cycle is governed by a performance ranking of the employees, which is known as "stack ranking." While some companies shy away from following such a rigid process as forced ranking, it is typically true that the higher performing employees get the larger portion of the available salary increases, while the lower performing employees get less and sometimes zero. Unless your company has a clear and easily understood alternative to this approach, it is likely that you are being ranked whether it is formally announced or not. The amount of funds available for salary increases is usually proportional to the health of the company. If the company is doing well, then a larger portion will be allocated, and if it is doing poorly, then fewer dollars will be available.

It is important that you understand that the total amount your firm allocates for company-wide salary increases on a given year may be outside of your day-to-day control. Some years they will allocate a large sum of funds, and some years they will not. The biggest impact you can have is to make sure that you do your job well, and that you know how to get yourself a comparatively good portion of the allocated funds. You should be analyzing your firm's financial performance every month or every quarter so that you understand the company's ability to fund increases. Is your firm making money? Is your team performing well compared with the firm's performance? Draw a line between your day-to-day success and how that is helping your company make money or reduce costs.

You should always remember that in most firms, salary increases are not a given right. They must be earned, and you will not receive an increase simply for showing up. Not only must you achieve successful outcomes, but you must also achieve them in such a way that they align with your firm's stated goals (such as customer satisfaction, revenue targets, or whatever they declare for the given period). Many professional services firms will focus heavily on having you demonstrate your successful outcomes in order to receive any increase. You need to know exactly what outcomes are expected of you so that you can prepare adequately for the performance review that precedes the salary increases.

Don't be the employee who walks into his or her supervisor's office expecting an 8% increase only to find out that you are getting nothing. Your performance review should *never* be a surprise. You should be talking constantly with your manager about your performance and your alignment with issues that matter. As we discussed in the *engaging with your career* section, you should also regularly assess yourself against the key performance indicators (KPI's) or measurable business objectives (MBO's) that have been assigned to you. Make sure that the definition of these metrics is clear. Ask for clarifications if you have questions about them. It does you no good to chase the wrong target all year. Meeting or surpassing your agreed success measurements is the best way to demonstrate your eligibility for a salary increase. Also, be aware of the progress other people are making towards their goals. Are most of your team members meeting their metrics? As unfortunate as it is, this is usually a comparative process, so it will do you good to understand where you might be ranked.

Don't be afraid to talk to your manager about the upcoming salary adjustments. Don't badger him or her, but it's worth asking for the list of outcomes necessary to achieve eligibility for an increase. Never put pressure on your manager by saying you "need" the increase. This is unlikely to work, and it will also highlight you as someone who is likely to exit voluntarily if you don't get it.

If You Aren't Awarded an Increase

You are undoubtedly disappointed. As frustrating as it might be, don't handle this frustration by taking it out on your manager or others in your work environment. It can damage your long-term standing with your manager and your employer. The news of this kind of dissent travels fast. If you need to take a day or two to cool down, then do so. The most important action for you to take is to sit down with your manager and determine the reasons why you were not ranked high enough to be awarded an increase.

Sometimes, the budget available to your manager simply couldn't be stretched to include all employees. Albeit little concern of yours, these are a horrible situation for a manager, so he or she is not going to feel good about it. If the reason is not that simple, and you were deliberately skipped, then this meeting may include some difficult feedback for you to hear. You may even disagree with some of it, but you must listen to it all the same because it is still worthwhile. In these circumstances, perception is reality, so even if you are perceived to have failed to demonstrate a behavior, at this stage, there is nothing you can do to reverse it, other than to seriously consider the value of the feedback.

In these circumstances, it is important to ask your manager if he or she could help solicit more anonymous feedback from other managers or peers so that you can get a complete picture of some of the characteristics that may be holding you back. I have been through a couple of these 360-degree feedback reviews, and the consistency and directness of the areas for improvement can be uncomfortable to hear.

However, it is often eye opening, and it typically motivates you toward improving the commonly identified areas of weakness. I thoroughly recommend the process.

These discussions should end with you having a full assessment of the behaviors that caused you to be overlooked for the salary increase. This is an incredibly valuable list to have, but only you can determine if you believe the assessment is accurate. I can't assure you that it will be, but I do know that if multiple people have identified the same weaknesses, then you will do well to work on strengthening them. Once you have made that assessment, you should sit with your manager and develop a training plan to try correcting them. Suggest adding them to your one-on-one discussion with your manager so that you constantly evaluate your progress. This will make a clear statement that you take the issue seriously, and that you want to correct the issues and achieve a salary increase on the next review cycle.

Nothing impresses me more than a person who didn't get an increase but then works hard at an agreed improvement plan. I've often gone out of my way to get approval for an out of cycle salary increase for people that demonstrate true commitment to improving their skills. Unfortunately, I can't guarantee that your manager will do the same, but I think your willingness to grow will earn you respect and should make you noticeable when the next increase cycle begins.

Summary: Understanding Salary Increases

If you don't get a salary increase, remember that every dark cloud has a silver lining. That silver lining may exist with your current employer or elsewhere, but rest assured, your situation is always recoverable in some way. If you stay with your current employer, be willing to listen and remain engaged with the program. If you move to another firm, be ready to switch gears and become engaged; otherwise the same process will repeat. Ultimately, you are the master of your destiny, so whatever you do, make your decisions when you are calm and rational, and only after you have considered all of the available information.

FIELD EXAMPLE: A REAL LIFE CAREER PATH

As a part of this chapter, I wanted to make sure that you heard from someone (other than me) about the impact *staying engaged* has had on their career. I once worked with a very bright guy from the UK named Nick Jones. He was a fantastically committed individual, and I could tell that he remained closely engaged with his job, the company, and his career.

He was very clear about his career path, and in our very first discussion, told me, "I would love to eventually have your job." Because I believed he had all the right skills to do so, I was very excited to learn of his ambitions. Although I haven't worked with Nick now for almost 5 years, I recently checked back in with him and found that he has proven himself every bit of the principle-led professional services executive I expected him to be. I encourage you to listen to his story as I think it is a great and somewhat typical path that those who are committed to staying engaged with their professional services careers can achieve.

"I got into consulting almost by accident. I started my career as an engineer for a startup software company and found that I gained more satisfaction from working directly with customers than with other engineers. In my first year as a consultant, I realized how informal a lot of our engagements were, and consequently, how much trouble we got ourselves into.

The engagements were frustrating and difficult, and I considered leaving. Do I stay with this new-found consulting thing, or do I just quit and go back to being an engineer? I made the decision to get engaged with my career and try to make a difference. I started to think more about my role in the company and how I could help it by doing my job better and looking for opportunities to step up to big challenges.

My first opportunity came when I identified myself as a candidate to save a failing project. I voluntarily developed a quality plan in the hopes of getting the doomed project back on track and our Director of Professional Services noticed my commitment. Later that month, I was promoted into the role of a team leader. Looking back on it, the connection was obvious: demonstrate a deeper understanding of the business of professional services and obtain customer results, and I will highlight myself as a candidate for promotion.

I knew that if I stayed committed to helping my customers be successful and communicated well with my managers, I would give myself the best chance of continued success. My next opportunity came a year later with a challenging project at a major UK bank. This customer had invested heavily with us, but after a yearlong engagement, we were nowhere near done, and the environment had soured. I was given the opportunity to turn it around. This was a clear opportunity for me to demonstrate my leadership skills and move into stage 4 of my career.

It became clear to me that the consultants on the engagement had fallen into the trap of failing to hold the customer accountable. They said 'yes' to everything the customer asked for without initiating any form of change control or challenging the benefit of the request. They also neglected to hold the customer accountable for the delays these requests were causing. My first task was to have difficult conversations with the customer's project team and explain the root causes of their issues. I had to say 'Yes, if...' to a lot of requests and make it clear that there were consequences for continually changing the definition of done. Eventually, I developed a new rescue plan and prescribed it to some of the reluctant customer stakeholders. As uncomfortable as it was, I had to tell them to take it or leave it. I had to leverage their fear of failure, and thankfully, it worked. After this success, I was soon the head of service delivery for the UK and Europe.

Once, in an attempt to find better career, I moved companies and this is where I met Shane. As a result of our conversations focused on my career we identified an opportunity for me to manage an offshore team of developers in a newly-formed center of excellence. This was a great opportunity to get involved with the company's collective wisdom and turn it into a revenue-generating product that delivered more reliable customer success. While it wasn't much of a promotion from what I was already doing, it was a global role instead of local, and it gave me a prime vantage point to survey the global landscape of my company and identify my next move.

Throughout this time, I stayed engaged in what my company was doing. I knew all of the executives, and they knew me. I didn't need to pester them with useless information or try to promote myself, I just needed to show them that I could achieve results, and I did. When that company was purchased, they cleared out a lot of my colleagues and friends. I could easily have left and not given *the new owners a chance, but I stayed patient. I could see that my role was pivotal to the new company's ability to make use of their new purchase. This gave me a great opportunity to demonstrate my capabilities.*

Within two years, I became the Director of Global Professional Services for my specific product line and moved into the job I had been planning for. I now run a large enterprise professional services business and a team of over 100 people. I still have plenty of plans for my future. I need to continue to execute against the principles and lead my team to growth. At all times, I stay engaged with my company, my team, and my customers. Without a doubt, my ability to stay engaged with my own career has been one of the key reasons I have managed to progress to where I am today. Staying engaged and carefully managing the direction of my own career has allowed me to control my own destiny and make the most of the opportunities that present themselves."

CHAPTER SUMMARY

A tightrope walker cannot afford to lose focus; otherwise, their walk may take an unexpected and irreversible detour. If something goes wrong, tightrope walkers may not be around to play the blame game, so they take matters into their own hands. They check their own rigs, they constantly assess their surroundings, and they receive and accept honest, effective feedback about their chances of conquering a death-defying challenge.

Thankfully, our jobs don't usually involve life and death decisions such as these, but as a professional services consultant, your career requires the same kind of intense focus. You must maintain control of your career and ensure that you know the direction of it at all times. *Get engaged* with your career or suffer the consequence of having others decide your fate. Maintain your focus on your career goals and how you intend to progress toward them. Keep awareness as to what is happening within your organization and your industry so you can assess your options. Bring your own experiences and thoughts to the table, and put your ideas into the mix. Eventually, you will learn what works for you and what doesn't. Regardless of the outcome, each attempt leaves you better for having tried. Even if you slip slightly on a career step, this principle will give you everything you need to recover quickly.

CONCLUSION:
THIS IS ONLY THE BEGINNING

"Obey the principles without being bound by them."

– Bruce Lee

I sincerely hope this book addressed several of the situations you face as a professional services consultant. I hope the dynamics and nuances I've described have become more apparent in your daily work. As these challenging situations continue to arise, you should attack them with the seven principles in mind. In the same way they have served others, they will surely serve you well.

To make them habitual, you must contemplate and discuss them regularly. Reading this book once will not permit you to master them. However, it will provide you with a framework that you can begin using today. But if you read it repeatedly and you commit the principles to memory, you're definitely on the right track. If you go beyond that and make them a part of your daily work, it is without question that you'll see positive results!

It is impossible to deliver each principle to perfection all of the time. Set a realistic expectation of how you will deliver and continue to increase the level of your expectations as you see improvements. Employing all of these principles together and delivering them in unison is difficult. If it were easy, there would be no need for this book. While I have employed these principles countless times throughout my career, I still miss opportunities to embrace them. Worse still, sometimes even when I employ them, I do so in a manner that falls short of my own high standards! Even after almost 20 years of delivering professional services, I can still sometimes find myself editing my own thoughtless statement after I have already said it, and then waiting too long to have the difficult conversation to correct it. However, aspirations and a dedication to self-improvement are what distinguish the extraordinary from the ordinary, and becoming extraordinary requires that you never fail to work toward achieving the goals you wish to obtain. Therefore, you should never give up!

Remember that every organization is different and your firm may have unique practices, and it is okay if some of your firm's practices are at odds with my recommendations. Discuss my advice with your manager, and ask them to help you better understand your firm's approach. This will demonstrate your eagerness to learn the industry, as well as your firm's approach within it. Some of the approaches I have recommended are specific to professional services being delivered for a profit, and they may neglect to account for other approaches to generating revenue (like the sale of hardware or software).

My advice may not apply directly to all types of professional services. The principles may need to be adjusted slightly based on your particular subject area, but I'm very confident that you will be able to identify the same patterns I have outlined and apply them to the specifics of your current circumstance. After all every customer who purchases a service is attempting to achieve the same thing -- a successful outcome. Once you have identified these patterns, you can also find a way to appropriately apply the principles, or adjust them to address what lies ahead. All of this will help you build a collective wisdom that will be valuable to both you and your firm.

Talk to your manager about the principles. Obtain the benefit of his or her experience. There are many great professional services executives in the industry, and you should lean on them for guidance and use them as a resource to help your career. Each executive will have his or her own take on these principles, and their experience in your industry may provide you with a more precise level of guidance. Together you can adopt an approach that will be right for your specific situation.

By the same token, talk to your colleagues about the principles. You are all out there fighting the same fight, trying to achieve similar goals. Even if you are talking to a professional services consultant from a competitive firm, you have a common experience that you can discuss in terms of these principles. You are both facing a common struggle, and conversing about these principles will allow you to focus on the respective issues and challenges you face. The more you discuss the principles as a group, the faster you will learn from the experiences of others and the faster you will employ them to achieve your customer's success.

The professional services industry can be demanding; there are many sacrifices that will occur for the greater good. Demanding clients and demanding schedules combine with considerable amounts of travel to create a level of stress that can be difficult to manage. There are many instances where you feel as though you're pushing uphill and sailing against the breeze, but when the rewards come, make sure that you reap them. As a professional services consultant, a job well done is as satisfying as any other work I've encountered.

Make sure that you are prepared to take the good with the bad. The world of a professional services consultant ebbs and flows. One minute it is insanely busy, and the next, you are twiddling your thumbs around the office for days. Enjoy the breaks. Learn something new and prepare yourself for the next customer engagement. Above all, make a serious effort to avoid the dreadful effects of burnout.

And finally, take encouragement from this chapter's opening quote. Bruce Lee's view of the principles of martial arts applies equally to the life of a professional services consultant. As these principles embody the wisdom of your predecessors, you must obey them. And yet, your particular circumstances are unique to you, and therefore, you cannot be entirely bound by them. Be creative in applying the wisdom of those who went before you, but don't hesitate to try new things and contribute to the wisdom of those who are sure to follow.

The principles exist only to serve you. It would be detrimental to make idols of them in the belief that it is your duty to serve them! In this book's final pages, Mr. Lee's statement provides wisdom for the final tightrope we must all walk. You cannot become a master until you believe whole-heartedly in the wisdom of the principles. Simultaneously, you must believe in yourself enough to know that you too are capable of wisdom, and therefore, you must tailor these principles to your circumstances in order to truly succeed. Learn the principles, but don't be overly constricted by my interpretation of them -- or anyone else's! Experience them, apply them, analyze them specific to your situation, and then trust in your own ability to adjust them when needed.

If, after reading all of this, you are still in the game (and I hope that you are), then I wish you all the best. The success of the teams I have managed, the relationships that I have built, and the friends I have made, are testimony enough that there is value in these principles, and there is incredible satisfaction in knowing you have delivered them well. Take these principles and apply them where you can, and I believe your career will be the better for having done so.

I believe wholeheartedly, that these principles belong to the industry, which now, makes you an active custodian of their collective wisdom. Like countless others, I have learned them from friends and peers, and I've lived with them for years. I've spent countless hours contemplating how to master them, how to teach them to others, and ultimately, how to articulate them in book form so that they can be corralled into one place for easier adoption.

I am not protective of them, nor am I territorial in their expression. They are neither frozen in time, nor are they immune to the effects of progress. As the industry evolves, so should the principles. If you find flaws in them, you must help us identify and overcome them by contributing your thoughts to the collective wisdom of our professional community. Feel free to be the person who challenges and improves these principles to our benefit!

Good Luck!

WWW.PSPRINCIPLES.COM

NOTES

NOTES

NOTES

24189121R00165

Made in the USA
Middletown, DE
17 September 2015